Piano:
GUIDED
Sight-Reading

Piano:
Guided
Sight-Reading

**A New Approach to
Piano Study**

Second Edition

Leonhard Deutsch

Nelson-Hall/Chicago

ISBN 0-88229-555-1 (cloth)
ISBN 0-88229-556-X (paperback)

10   9   8   7   6   5   4   3

Acknowledgements

For the constructive criticism and final editing of my manuscript I wish to express my gratitude and appreciation to Miss Lillian Cooper, New York City. For the patient reading of the first drafts and helpful suggestions my thanks go to the late Mrs. Sophia Steinbach, New York City; Miss Ruth Norden, New York City; and Mr. & Mrs. Horace Champney, Yellow Springs, Ohio. Finally, I have to thank Crown Publishers for the last retouches.

For their adherence to my ideas abroad and in this country I thank my former Vienna colleagues and co-workers Dr. Alexander Klahr, New York City; Mr. Victor Popper, Evanston, Illinois; Mrs. Maria Treuer, Yellow Springs, Ohio; and Dr. Margaret Wolf, Brooklyn, N.Y.

I feel greatly indebted to my wife, Mrs. Danica Deutsch, for her most active support of my work from its very beginning. She also assisted me in applying experiences from her own field, including her study of left-eyedness, to the psychological and emotional problems of my students.

LEONHARD DEUTSCH

Contents

CONTENTS

Foreword

"A NEW approach to piano study? Why?" the reader may well ask. "Hasn't the old approach produced hundreds and thousands of excellent pianists?"

True, for such successful students, usually professional musicians, no change is necessary; but for the others, less fortunate, the legions of lay musicians, playing the piano can acquire a new meaning.

Formerly the non-professional pianist had the same mission as the virtuoso: to share his musicianship with an audience. And usually he was just as eager for publicity. He labored many hours over technical exercises and spent years building a repertoire of pieces carefully prepared for performance.

Nowadays such toil hardly seems worth while. Since radio and phonograph bring first-rate performance at any time to any place, who is interested in listening to an amateur's playing? Indeed, when radio and phonograph became part of our civilization, many people warned that the days of amateur music were numbered. The opposite happened, however. Today non-professional music study is more widespread than ever before. An apparent contradiction, but the explanation is simple.

Since more people listen to more music, particularly to serious music, many listeners want to play that music—to play it for their own pleasure. A person who plays himself, even if he is far from perfect, is rewarded by a sense of satisfaction that mere listening cannot supply.

Conversely, he will be a better listener if he plays, for many a detail escapes those who depend on ear alone.

"To play for one's own pleasure"—with this goal, traditional methods are seldom compatible. Spending weeks if not months on every piece in order to perfect it is not enjoyment of music. It is drudgery. For many decades multitudes of amateur students have taken piano lessons with great expectations. Most of them had to give up soon, as they could not achieve any repertoire at all. Yet even the more successful amateurs came to feel that their repertoire had demanded too much of them and had given too little in return. It embraced only a tiny fraction of all music literature, and those students were deprived of rich musical nourishment and of an opportunity to explore. Their accomplishments were short-lived. Dependent on a teacher's aid, they worked only for as long as they took lessons. After they dropped their teachers, they hardly ever forged ahead and usually they quickly forgot what they had learned.

These failures were not inevitable. They could have been avoided if students had been taught *to read at sight*.

Sight-reading is a skill which offers a student access to all music literature; a skill through which he can acquaint himself with any composition, unaided by a teacher.

Nor can the ability to sight-read be lost. Once musical notation has become a living picture for the student, it will remain so, and he will at any time afterward be able to perform any music whether he practices regularly or not.

Sight-reading does not conflict with repertoire study. On the contrary, a good sight-reader has no trouble in perfecting a piece, and is all the more stimulated to do so.

After a student has developed adequate facility in sight-reading, he is ready for unrehearsed or little rehearsed performance; this is especially important for chamber musicians and accompanists. Also, to musicians in other fields who take piano lessons as an additional subject, sight-reading will be very welcome.

Thus it is suitable for every piano pupil. For the amateur student, however, the sight-reading method is imperative. Not only does it direct him to an appropriate goal—developing musicianship—but it also helps him to attain it. It is not the privilege of specially talented persons. To play a piano piece correctly at sight implies nothing more than a coordination of the player's ears, eyes, and hands. Every normal person can develop that coordination, though it may mean hard work for some.

The efficacy of sight-reading has been proven by my own teaching experience and by that of my co-workers over a period of a great many years with numerous students of all ages and types. Most of our students would have failed under traditional instruction. Many actually *had* failed, but they resumed their piano studies with our new approach and then succeeded.

We certainly did not expect to, nor did we, make brilliant pianists of our amateur students. What we did find was that the sight-reading program helped every one of them to extend steadily his musical and technical abilities, his knowledge of the master works of music, and his power of discrimination. It deepened the student's love of serious music and quickened his enthusiasm for the piano.

These are the results an amateur with only limited time for piano study may reasonably aim at, and they are indeed no mean achievements.

Piano:
GUIDED
Sight-Reading

The Story of the Sight-Reading Method

THE sight-reading method, as described in this book, departs completely from the conventional methods of piano instruction. Whoever has experience in usual methods very likely will be prejudiced against the new concept of piano study and find it rather difficult to follow and accept. In order to make myself more easily understood and to prepare my reader for the theory of the sight-reading method, I should like to set down the development of my ideas. It is the story of a revolution which sprang from a great personal disappointment.

My pianistic career started like that of thousands of other students. My piano lessons began when I was eight.

All I had known of music before that were the songs I had learned in school and the popular "hits" I heard played by street organs—at that time the main sources of music for the average city child. Then I was told that a world of heavenly tonal beauty existed, more enchanting by far than my trivial musical experiences, and that this world was open only to music students.

With the expectation of heavenly tones, I met my piano teacher. He received me with an equally definite, though quite different expectation: he wanted to make a virtuoso of me. He had tested my musical ear and my hands and pronounced me to have a great talent.

The discrepancy in our expectations was bound to disappoint both my teacher and me. My own disappointment appeared in the very first lesson, when my teacher started out with finger exercises, scales, and other drills, dry as dust. This remained my musical diet for a considerable time. Later my teacher assigned dull études—by Cramer, Clementi, Czerny, and others—while, for recreation, I was allowed to work on shallow "recital pieces for young people."

Whenever I complained about all this stuff, my teacher put me off with the promise that real music would soon follow, that I had to prepare technically for my reward by working faithfully on these less pleasant preliminary assignments.

My disillusionment grew when I arrived at sonatinas and other pieces by uninspired composers—Bertini, Diabelli, Kohler, Kuhlau, etc.—music that was almost as devoid of beauty as the savorless études and exercises.

What bored me even more than the mediocre music was the way I had to handle it. My teacher had me play each new piece at sight under his supervision, so that I might gain an over-all impression. Actually, he made me terribly nervous, sitting beside me, watching my hands, being ever alert to correct me. I had to count the beats throughout, and this hindered me so much in deciphering the notes that I stumbled over notes as well as over the counting. My well-meaning teacher interrupted me constantly even to correct my fingering. He marked my mistakes liberally over the page, together with suggestions and warnings. Now my music, littered with finger guides and marks of all kinds, sizes, and colors, appeared to me like a battlefield and filled me with horror.

This was my "over-all impression" of the piece.

4

For homework I was instructed to break the piece into small bits, and separate the parts of each hand. I was to repeat each fraction alone many times, then piece the bits together gradually. Finally I had to repeat the reassembled piece until a perfect, glib mastery of it was achieved.

I was kept many weeks on a piece before I was allowed to glimpse a new one. Also, I had to go through all my completed pieces regularly in order to build up a "repertoire" and keep it intact.

Very likely I would have given up had I not one day run across an album of classical piano pieces which a visitor had left in our home. I skimmed through the book and attempted to play some of the pieces. Most of them were too far advanced for a pupil who had been playing for only two years, but I succeeded with two easier pieces: *Fantasy in D Minor,* by Mozart, and *Mazurka in G Minor* op. 67 No. 2, by Chopin.

This time my playing at sight did indeed help me to get an over-all impression of those pieces despite my clumsiness and blunders, for I was absorbed in the music, not distracted by counting out the time and observing the fingering, nor bothered by my teacher's interference with my playing.

And this time the impression was overwhelming. Mozart's *Fantasy* stirred me like a wonderful drama with a triumphant ending. Chopin's nostalgic mazurka filled me with romantic sentiment. Never before had I heard such music, yet I knew that this was the kind of enchantment I had imagined when, two years earlier, I had been told glorious musical adventure awaited me.

I could not help playing these pieces over and over, giving no attention to performance, fascinated only by the music.

During the next lesson I played these pieces exultantly for my teacher. He did not share my elation! In fact he was some-

5

what nonplussed. He sharply criticized my wretched performance and declared that these pieces were far beyond my technical ability and that I must wait at least two years more for such
music.

Arguments flared after that, and eventually were settled by a
compromise. My teacher consented to study such a "premature"
piece with me occasionally, while I promised to follow his "regular" assignments.

I had promised too much. It was impossible for me to wait
until my teacher doled out a piece of "my" music. Music stores
and lending libraries offered an abundance of the music I craved
—the works of the great masters. More and more I neglected my
teacher's assignments, nor did I attempt to perfect the pieces of
my own choice. After all, I had no intention of impressing anyone with my playing. All I aimed at was to enjoy the music that
thrilled me. I did extract enjoyment even out of my shiftless
performance and was unperturbed by minor mistakes and slips.

After many rows with my teacher he grudgingly capitulated.
He put up with my failure to perfect even one single repertoire
piece. But he did not give me up, as he still firmly believed in
my talent. He did not doubt that my talent would bloom and
flourish some day, the day when I would listen to reason and
follow his suggestions.

I did not want to give up my teacher, as I had a good reason
for staying with him: I depended upon his help when I had
trouble in deciphering a new piece.

In this way we jogged along for a number of years. I was
seventeen when I parted ways with my teacher. He had lost all
hope for me, and I had become independent of his help. By
then I could play any music that pleased me—mostly of classic
and romantic style—and I kept on exploring music literature
in my informal way.

6

At college age I became an eager concert-goer. I was interested in all kinds of concerts, but most fascinated by the recitals of soloists, particularly violinists and pianists—Ysaÿe, Hubermann, Flesch, Burmester, Kubelik, Rosenthal, Sauer, D'Albert, Godowsky, Friedmann, to mention a few. Their brilliant performances made me feel ashamed of my own poor pianistic achievements, and I turned from my simply musical interest to pianistic art.

To be sure, I did not dream of competing with virtuosi. I had no desire to show off. But I realized that professional handling of the piano would gratify me far more than my amateurish playing.

I decided to attempt to perfect at least a small standard repertoire. Conquering my dislike of the conventional practicing routine, I returned repentantly to the expedients which my teacher had formerly suggested in vain.

My surprise was boundless when I came to see that these expedients were ineffective! I observed the printed fingering, labored on every detail of a piece, kept on repeating each piece, and still my technique failed to show any considerable improvement.

I saw only one more resource: the hated technical drills. I studied the vast literature on piano mechanics, and with all my self-conquest went through the ordeal suggested in these books. I found no help!

Before very long I closed my piano in surrender, with no intention of opening it again. Also, I avoided piano recitals, and went only to opera, and to orchestra and chamber music concerts.

This was how I came to make a great discovery: Johann Sebastian Bach.

As a piano student, I had no concern with Bach despite all

I knew about him from hearsay. My teacher had assigned to me a number of Bach pieces, but had mostly stressed fussy ornaments and still more fussy fingering. Later I had sporadically attempted to play Bach in my own way, disregarding ornaments and fingering; but I found, without knowing why, that I could not manage this style at all. So I had put the Bach albums on the shelf.

Now, during this concert-going period, when a friend invited me to join him in attending Bach's *St. Matthew's Passion,* I followed rather reluctantly, because I still remembered my fruitless efforts at the piano. But no sooner had the orchestra started the introduction, than I was seized by a feeling of rapture I had never experienced before. This feeling stayed with me during the four hours' performance and for days afterwards.

The first thing I did when I woke from the trance and found myself back on earth was buy the piano score of the divine masterpiece and play it. This time I had no trouble managing Bach's music, and so I felt encouraged to take the *Welltempered Clavichord* from my shelf.

This work, however, still resisted my efforts. But now I was too eager and would not abandon it again. Where there's a will there's a way—and indeed I soon found a way to manage the intricacies of Bach's counterpoint: I simply slowed down the tempo to far below the speed an actual performance would require. This restraint helped me render the pieces accurately and evenly, and I found I could ignore the printed fingering.

I tried more of Bach's piano music, enjoying it even at the unusual slow tempo. Before very long I experienced another reward: I was gradually gaining fluency without depending on numerous repetitions of each piece. Also I developed a degree of security in my fingers which I never had felt before.

Then it occurred to me that this improvement meant tech-

8

nique! I wondered whether I could transfer my new facility to other pianistic styles—Schumann, Chopin, Brahms, etc. It worked! I played these compositions at sight without any break, giving accuracy first importance and retarding my tempo. When I repeated a piece several times in the same manner, I observed a gain in fluency without any loss of ease, accuracy, or finger control. Eventually, without changing this routine or adding anything to it, I was able to play the piece with full élan.

My conclusion, paradoxical as it sounded, was correct: technique is developed by slowing down the practicing tempo, not by speeding it up as I had done before.

By my new type of piano work I was even more inspired than by my former foot-loose adventure in the classics. With boredom completely absent from my practicing hours, I soon built up a large repertoire. But I was not so much interested in my technique as in the way I had achieved it. For I believed that I had found a simple and effective method of studying the piano that would supersede the conventional tedious and ineffective routine. I felt confident that my new route to pianistic facility would work with everybody as it had worked with me, and I decided to share my discovery with the more or less advanced amateur pianists among my friends and acquaintances. They were about my age, not particularly gifted, and had eagerly studied the piano for a number of years, but, unlike me, had confined themselves to repertoire study, adhering to the traditional rules of practicing.

I suggested that they learn their next new pieces in the same manner as I did. I took it for granted that everyone could achieve accuracy and evenness, if only he played slowly enough. I just wondered whether repetition would help to increase other students' speed as it had my own.

This question, however, was not answered by my first experiments, since, to my astonishment, none of my guinea pigs, in tackling and repeating a piece as a whole, could manage accuracy and evenness, no matter how slowly they played. Thus I realized that the primary problem of these students was *to learn to play at sight accurately and evenly.*

With this new objective in mind I continued my experiments, working with these and other students, but for a while without any positive result, until a fortunate incident came to my aid. Once, while working with a high-strung student whose attempts at sight-reading reflected his nervous tension, I felt the desire to join him in playing, though I remembered how my own teacher had made me nervous by his habit of playing along with me in the higher octave registers. With this student, however, the same procedure worked the other way: he calmed down and his sight-reading improved considerably.

I tried accompaniment with other students and in various ways. Some students responded immediately, some after a few attempts; some very slightly, some not at all. Yet the best a responsive student gained was accuracy and evenness, not speed. I had to admit that my "streamlined" method of repertoire study was limited to myself.

Nevertheless I was not completely disappointed by these experiments. They turned my interest from repertoire to sight-reading as a goal, and my initial successes toward this new goal were encouraging, especially as my students, too, became greatly interested in sight-reading.

I continued working with them and with new students and decided to devote myself entirely to teaching. No longer did I expect to achieve miracles, especially when I saw that many students adhered to their ineffectual working habits and disregarded my suggestions and guidance. Also, a number of students who did follow instruction and who seemed to be getting along nicely nevertheless gave up for no apparent reason.

Thus I understood that a piano teacher dealing with the average student could not simply offer suggestions and leave it to the student to regard or disregard them. It was not out of defiance but rather out of weakness that a student failed to cooperate with me, and I felt called upon to help the student overcome this weakness.

I owe it to my great teacher Alfred Adler and his school of *Individual Psychology* that I learned to understand the weaknesses of any given pupil, to draw conclusions from his working habits about his whole personality, and to help him achieve readjustment. It took me many years and much trial and error to elaborate the generally effective system of guided sight-reading described in this book.

I have used this method since the 1920's with well over 300 students. Half of them carried on for at least one year and up to eight years; their average was two years. Among the permanent students 15 per cent were children (ages 8 to 12), 25 per cent young adolescents (12 to 16), 25 per cent from 16 to 25, 20 per cent from 25 to 40, and 15 per cent over 40. Among the children there was an equal number of boys and girls; with increasing age the female sex outnumbered the male:

12 to 16: 2 f to 1 m
16 to 25: 3 f to 1 m
25 to 40: 5 f to 1 m
over 40: 8 f to 1 m

Twenty per cent of all my students were novices; the others had followed conventional methods for a considerable time (at least one year, up to fifteen years), but had arrived at a dead point and continued (or resumed) piano work only because they trusted the sight-reading method. Forty per cent of the pretrained students had to start sight-reading from the very begin-

11

ning; 50 per cent showed some facility, and only 10 per cent had a considerable pianistic and musical background.

To my own experience was added that of my co-workers and followers. We introduced our method to the public in Vienna in 1926. From then to 1938 we held weekly meetings to which we invited students, demonstrated their responses and achievements, and discussed their problems. Thus, exchanging our experiences, each of us could observe progress and results in the work of hundreds of students year by year. We also interviewed and tested many visitors, who told of their experiences with conventional piano instruction and eagerly let us ascertain their abilities and their shortcomings.

A detailed report of these weekly demonstrations and of our teaching experiences would fill a large volume. But neither a volume of case histories nor a collection of statistics is necessary to prove the effectiveness of our sight-reading method, since ample proof was, and is, offered by the progress of *every* student. Most striking are the results of those who took up sight-reading only after they had more or less unsuccessfully followed conventional methods.

Nonetheless the problems of teaching are not solved simply by working out an effective pedagogic technique. There still remains the task of coping with a student's personality—the problem of overcoming his resistance to work and to instruction.

Unfortunately the percentage of these maladjusted students is rather high. Therefore, the future of teaching lies not only in improved teaching methods but also in better psychological training of teachers, and in the proper training of parents to enable them to bring up better-adjusted children.

The Problems of Sight-Reading

THE groundwork for piano instruction as we know it today was laid in the beginning of the nineteenth century. From the outset, repertoire was stressed; playing at sight was neglected. Many students developed a considerable facility in playing, but it was limited to the repertoire pieces which they carefully worked out. We still meet many students who perform well a polonaise by Chopin perhaps, but cannot decipher an easy sonata by Haydn.

Only those students have learned to sight-read who have done in at their own initiative. They did not confine themselves to their teachers' assignments, but played in addition a much larger volume of music of their own choice. They started with simple pieces and, in the course of many years, worked up to music of ever growing difficulty.

Incidentally, there are good sight-readers who have never taken formal lessons or worked on repertoire.

This suggests that sight-reading be made a required subject in piano study, rather than allowed to depend on the student's initiative. In fact, today's progressive teachers do attempt to carry out this idea. They have every student acquire some sight-reading facility by working out a repertoire and then assign sight-reading material that is easier than the repertoire pieces which the student has just mastered. From there on, he is expected to proceed with sight-reading material parallel to the increasing difficulty of his repertoire pieces.

However, the problems of sight-reading cannot be solved that easily.

In the first place, the vast majority of piano pupils fail in their repertoire work and have to give up their studies altogether before they have a chance to attempt sight-reading. Even among the fairly successful repertoire students there are many who are unable to read at sight the simplest pieces in a tolerable manner. They grope their way with much stumbling and stammering, frequently becoming confused. They do not improve by repeating their pieces or by expanding their material. Their sight-reading deteriorates in proportion to the increasing difficulty of their material.

Such efforts to read music can make a student feel uneasy and troubled. It is no wonder that most students have never had the initiative to sight-read on their own. Sight-reading is not merely a matter of determination and persistence; therefore it is useless to suggest sight-reading exercises to a student who tackles them incorrectly. His practicing would only discourage him and he would give up soon.

What is the correct way to practice sight-reading?

Above all, we must keep in mind that sight-reading which serves to develop the student's skill differs essentially from customary sight-reading, which is the application of a player's already developed skill. A pianist usually is called "a good sight-reader" if he can perform pieces perfectly or nearly perfectly without having previously studied them. For this purpose fluency and speed matter more than precision if the player covers up his minor inaccuracies and lapses.

Such sight-reading, however, can be only the *result* of exercises, not the exercises themselves. A student without sight-reading experience cannot, at first sight, play a piece both correctly and fluently.

To develop the skill of sight-reading, a student should at first aim not for speed but for *accuracy and evenness*. There are students who sight-read quite fluently, but their playing is sloppy and filled with mistakes; this procedure never leads to accurate sight-reading.

Sight-reading must be practiced with perfect precision, even at the cost of fluency and speed. We recommend a slow-motion rendition, so to speak, of a correct performance.

How is the ability to practice sight-reading in this manner developed?

Not necessarily through repertoire work. A pupil can—and usually does—perfect a piece by working at first on its details. He achieves accuracy and evenness after he has expended effort in numerous repeated drills over a considerable period of time. But to play a piece accurately and evenly at first sight requires the student's utterly concentrated effort. Students who develop the skill of sight-reading by themselves evidently did muster the necessary concentration; otherwise they would not have found the correct approach to sight-reading nor would they have felt any desire to carry on. Most students shun concentrated effort, but every student has a chance to overcome this difficulty with a teacher's help.

But none of the expedients teachers have employed in repertoire work is helpful for sight-reading. We know four of these expedients:

1. Repetition. The pupil repeats each piece over and again until he masters it.
2. Dissection. The pupil practices the part and fractions of a piece separately, and bit by bit reassembles them.
3. Imitation. The teacher plays the piece or a smaller unit of it to the pupil, and the latter tries to do the same.
4. Description. The teacher gives the pupil a precise set of rules and directions.

The first and the second of these expedients help a pupil grasp a pianistic task gradually, not spontaneously as he must in sight-reading.

The third[1] and fourth expedients require as much concentration as sight-reading does itself and therefore are not usable by a student who lacks the necessary concentration. Like a person too weak to walk by himself, he is not helped if walking is demonstrated or explained to him; he needs a guide who will walk with him and support him.

The most effective way to help a student in sight-reading, we have found, is *to join in his playing*. The teacher takes the lead and the student is advised to play along. Some students adjust themselves very soon to their teachers' playing, others only after a period of practicing.

With ensemble playing, another principle of instruction is established, the principle of *cooperation,* in which the pupil combines listening and playing simultaneously. This principle is effective with every pupil and every task.

To read a new piece, practice and experience are required. Joint sight-reading offers the student this experience. The teacher, by playing with his student, can control the latter's

[1] For a set of rules for sight-reading see pages 64 and 65.

method of practicing so that the student, practicing himself, will do so correctly.

What is the effect of sight-reading exercises?

As soon as a student has overcome the initial difficulties of sight-reading, he will progress steadily. After he has worked on study material of a certain degree of difficulty, he can manage material in the next grade without increased trouble. No one arrives at a standstill as long as he keeps working, and sight-reading is indeed stimulating enough to keep a student working.

Sight-reading exercises help a student not only to develop facility in playing music at sight, but also pianistic skill in general.

This should encourage the many students who cannot achieve mastery of the piano through repertoire study. For them, and actually for every piano student, sight-reading should be far more than an additional subject; it is basic training.

The following chapters should indicate how the different components of pianistic skill are developed by sight-reading.

The Basis of Pianistic Skill

1. MUSICAL EAR AND MANUAL DEXTERITY

THE roots of pianistic skill are musical ear and manual dexterity.

For a long time these qualities were considered inborn. If this were true, persons born without these qualities had no chance at all of developing pianistic skill and could not be helped by any method whatsoever. Yet the innateness of musical ear and manual dexterity has never been proved. The fact that a piano student fails is no evidence that he lacks the necessary predisposition; the fault may lie instead in the kind of instruction.

Today it is believed that pianistic aptitude is inborn to a certain extent or in certain cases, even though there is no way to find out to what extent and in what cases. It is quite fruitless to trace pianistic skill to heredity, and we should look for other sources.

First of all, we should examine the essence of musical ear and of manual dexterity, for neither of them is a simple and well-established entity.

19

What is musical ear?

A person is said to have musical ear, or to be musical, if he *understands* music. But music can be understood in various ways: one can understand the *feeling* that a piece of music expresses; one can realize how a given piece of music is *constructed* out of its elements; one can recognize the *style* and the *artistic value* of a composition.

Yet, first of all, we have to understand music by grasping its *meaning;* more exactly, the specifically *musical* meaning, since music may have meaning also in relation to words, sung or spoken, to a dance, a "program" or proceedings on the stage or on the screen.

The ability to grasp the specifically musical meaning of a composition is exactly what we call "musical ear."

This term is misleading, since we don't actually hear music with the ear. The auditory organ has no function other than to receive the tones and convey them to the mind. Grasping musical meaning is a far more *active* experience.

The musical meaning of a composition is inherent in its *totality.* Slight alterations of details, even single notes, can greatly change the meaning of a piece; yet the meaning can essentially be preserved in spite of considerable changes in details.

In order to understand a composition as a meaningful whole, we must mentally integrate its tones. When we listen to a piece of music which we immediately understand, our mental activity in integrating the tones is automatic and requires no perceptible effort. Then we are not aware of our activity, and our purely acoustic impression and the musical meaning are completely amalgamated in our mind. Thus it appears to us that we "hear" the music. Actually we hear only the tones. Similarly, we do not "hear" talk and its words and sentences; we hear merely a sequence of spoken sounds. It is our mind which integrates them into units and gives them meaning.

When we integrate tones into music, we understand the interrelation of the tones. The relation of coinciding tones ("vertical" relation) is called "harmony." The relation of subsequent tones ("horizontal" relation) comprises rhythm and melodic lines. The combination of both vertical and horizontal relations includes the trend of harmony as well as polyphony. Finally, the unity of all these musical elements in a piece is called "form" or "architecture."

Are some "ears" better than others? The answer is yes.

To an entirely unmusical person—of whom there are few in our civilization—music sounds like a conglomeration of tones. Such a person discriminates only the outer means of musical expression—tone-colors, movement, dynamics, and rhythm—and he receives these expressions only sporadically.

A listener with a rudimentary developed musical ear may grasp the leading melodic lines of a musical structure, but receives rather vague impressions of the harmony, polyphony, and form.

The musical ear of a well-trained person is measured by the complexity of the musical structure which he can grasp in all details.

Music in our Western civilization has developed from simple tonal relations to an ever-growing complexity, and parallel to this historic evolution, the musician's ear has developed.

In grasping the meaning of a composition, not only integration but also another activity is involved, namely, *expectation*. A musical person follows a piece of music with a certain degree of anticipation even when he hears it for the first time. Tones which contradict his expectation are felt to be "strange" or "false." A piece which goes beyond the limits of his understanding does not evoke his definite expectations; he calls this piece "too complicated," "meaningless," or "chaotic."

An unmusical person follows music indiscriminately without any anticipations. He does not distinguish between correct and false notes, or between simple and complicated structure.[1]

How is musical ear developed?

Were musical ear a congenital quality of certain privileged persons, these would develop it almost automatically, while the unmusical would be those who are "tone-deaf" from birth and definitely excluded from music.

Yet, as we have stated before, the musical ear has the job of integrating the tones into meaningful units. This is a mental skill which, like other skills, is developed through practicing. For this purpose, however, merely *listening* to music is inadequate. True, our mind follows music actively when we listen, but only to the degree to which our musical ear is already developed. A person, for example, whose ear is developed just to that degree which enables him to understand the style of Haydn and Mozart perfectly, does not by mere listening learn to understand the harmonic and other structural intricacies of the Romantic styles. Even repeated listening can result in no more than a superficial understanding. To grasp perfectly and in fullest detail the meaning of a musical structure which is too complicated for him, a person must intensify his mental activity: he has to *reproduce* that structure.

[1] Incidentally, musical understanding is not dependent on the possession of absolute pitch. There are many highly musical persons who lack that ability It probably rests upon the recognition of keys and subtle shades of their moods.

22

Reproducing music is also the most effective way of *awakening* the musical ear.

The simplest and most natural start in musical training is *singing,* usually learned during infancy and childhood, when the individual's faculty for imitation is most effective.

Every normal human being is potentially able to learn to sing, just as everyone is potentially able to learn to speak. Everybody learns to sing the kind of music his environment offers him, just as everybody learns his mother tongue. By speaking, a child learns to understand language; likewise, by singing, he learns to understand music. When a child is brought up in an environment where words are sparse, he will not easily learn to speak or to understand a language. Similarly, a child lacking musical environment will not develop a musical ear, though later he can make up for his deficiency by singing. However, with age an unmusical person finds it harder and harder to start singing. That does not mean that his musical predisposition degenerates, but indicates that the child's faculty of imitation deteriorates with maturity.

When a child learns many expressive songs, he develops deep musical emotions, love of music, and the desire to express himself musically. This fact sheds light upon the origin of musical families and musical nations. Their musicality is based not on heredity but on tradition. With them musical ear is not the cause but rather the consequence of their music-making.

Through singing, only a sense of melody and rhythm is cultivated, and this is but the *beginning* of ear-training.

The next step includes the understanding of harmony, polyphony, and larger forms. This understanding, too, is developed through reproducing music.

Several opportunities for reproducing polyphonic music are available. One is ensemble-playing or singing in a choir. While

23

playing or singing in a group, an instrumentalist or singer grasps the music as a whole by listening to the other parts and relating them to his own part. This is a rather difficult way to train the ear.

Another way to grasp polyphonic music as a whole is *reading its notation* with eye alone, without producing sound. Silent note-reading, too, is a kind of reproduction, though it is merely an internal experience. Facility in note-reading is part and parcel of musical education. By note-reading we learn to coordinate the heard or imagined sound to its notation. This coordination usually is developed by playing on a musical instrument from notes. When an instrumentalist plays music at sight, he can afterward read its notation silently. But it is rather hard immediately to read silently a notation which appears too complicated to the reader. On the other hand, there are persons, among them conductors and musicologists, who though they may not have mastered any musical instrument *can* read any musical score however complicated. They have chosen the most difficult method of ear-training.

The simplest way to grasp the meaning of polyphonic music is *to play it on a keyed instrument.* It follows that piano study would be the easiest course in advanced ear-training. A successful piano student then owes his highly developed musical ear to his piano study and not to his very earliest musical training.

A piano student, beginner or advanced, grasps the meaning of a composition, which is not too far beyond his comprehension, by playing it several times from notation. He must, of course, render it correctly, faithful to notes and rhythm. The other qualities of playing—expression and speed—do not matter for this purpose.

A student who is taught by the usual methods works on his pieces to the point of perfection, this task taking the greater part of his practicing time. He can spend very little time in acquainting himself with new music. Thus his musical development is retarded. This holds true particularly for plodding pupils.

A beginner with a poorly developed musical ear, who takes up the usual piano lessons, rarely has a chance to cultivate a better understanding of music, a better musical ear. For these students, special methods of ear-training have been suggested in recent years. Schematic drills have been assigned, which are supposed to help a student grasp single musical elements, such as intervals, chords, or rhythms. In addition, theory, including musical structure, is explained to the student.

In the writer's experience with students, however, nothing has proved so effective as playing the music as a whole, though simply.

Teachers who give it an honest try will find that *sight-reading* is the most effective method of ear-training. It helps all students, including those who have inadequate musical development, to cultivate a musical ear steadily.

What is manual dexterity?

Having analyzed one component of pianistic skill, musical ear, let us now consider the other.

Manual dexterity, generally speaking, is the ability to move the hands and fingers successfully for a definite purpose. The purpose of finger movements on the keyboard is to render music. Thus, *pianistic dexterity is the ability to coordinate hand and finger movements to music.*

A single movement in piano playing does not call for any particular dexterity at all; every layman can place his finger on a key and strike it.[1] What pianistic dexterity implies is not the single movement, but a proper *combination* of finger movements that will help to render the music.

How does manual skill develop?

Manual dexterity develops through *practicing*. "To practice" means to keep on doing designated purposeful movements. In the beginning these movements may miss their purpose or achieve it only after some delay. But with growing practice they become faster, more secure, and eventually automatic.

Manual dexterity is not a quality in itself, *detached* from purpose. Developed in one field, manual dexterity cannot be transferred to another field. Facility in needlework, for example, does not prepare a person for playing the piano, and piano practice is no preparation for learning to typewrite.

Pianistic dexterity is developed by practicing the coordination of hand and finger movements to music; in short, by playing it. This training hardly depends on a particular predisposition, since even *combinations* of finger movements on the keyboard require nothing unusual; in our everyday life we accomplish numerous combinations of finger movements that are still more intricate. Why then do most piano students fail to develop pianistic dexterity?

Now, to combine movements properly, we must be conscious of their purpose. It is our image of the purpose that helps us integrate our single movements into a whole and thus manage a coherent chain of movements. A person could not even put on or take off his coat if he were merely told, however accurately, what movements he should make, and were not told for what purpose.

[1] But a particular dexterity is necessary to strike two or more keys simultaneously with one hand and with different strength. (See footnote on page 53.)

26

To combine properly his finger movements on the keyboard, a player must be conscious of their purpose. That is, he must grasp as a whole the musical meaning of the piece he is to play. If he does not understand the interrelation of the tones in their entirety, he has trouble in connecting his finger movements. In spite of repetitions, they remain jittery and slow, and many will miss their aims.[1]

That is why an unmusical student is pianistically inept. If a *musical* student has failed to develop pianistic dexterity, we may be sure that he has not practiced effectively. He may have tried to separate his technical (hand) from his musical (ear) training; or he may have had an inadequate approach to practicing; or he may have limited his training to a much too small volume of study material.

In some of the following sections (on fingering, velocity, and finger agility) we shall discuss effective and ineffective approaches to practicing. Then we shall also see that the ideal combination of musical and technical training is offered by sight-reading exercises.

2. NOTES AND KEYS

Piano playing has been jestingly defined as "the art of hitting the right key at the right moment." This saying contains a grain of truth. Playing the correct notes and rhythms is the beginning of pianistic art and is indeed the minimum that we expect of a piano student.

In musical notation the keys which are to be played and the

---

[1] Likewise, a typist can type fluently only if he follows the meaning of the text as a whole. If he copies a text in a language which he does not understand, he has trouble finding the keys, familiar as he may be with his typewriter. His work is slower and less accurate than when he is handling a meaningful text.

time to play them are indicated precisely. So it would seem that anyone who knows the peculiarities of notation and those of the keyboard should be able to play any music at sight. Why should this be true in rare cases only? Why are many piano pupils, having followed the conventional method for years, still unable to read music, though they have no trouble recognizing notes and keys?

The reason is to be found in a method of instruction which requires a pupil to learn to recognize the keys of the instrument and the printed notes by their names and then practice playing from notation, picking out the keys note by note.

In a similar way school teachers formerly introduced children to the art of reading. At first the child learned the alphabet. Then he practiced combining letters, forming syllables and words, then sentences, and finally larger units.

This procedure, however, is quite different from actual reading. When we read, we do not grasp the letters one by one, but we take in the picture of a phrase or sentence as a whole and spontaneously grasp its meaning. We do not concentrate on the letters or syllable individually.

After a child has learned to recognize the letters and assemble them, he is still far from being able to read, that is, to grasp the meaning of the assembled letters. In order to learn to read, the child has to undergo another training process. This second course of training—discovering the meaning of writing—is not a continuation of the first—assembling letters. The second process does not depend on the first, and, as educators have demonstrated, can be learned without the alphabetical method. Modern teachers start by having the novice read whole sentences instead of detached letters and syllables. In this way he learns more quickly than he would by the alphabetical method, and he is spared a great deal of boring drill.

28

In language instruction the alphabetical method proved to be a detour; nevertheless, it did help every pupil eventually to learn to read.

Why is the alphabetical method, applied to music reading, ineffective?

The reason is simple: music does not have an alphabet.

Notes are not alphabetical units; their names are only a matter of convenience and do not relate to the musical meaning of notation. In language a letter represents a sound, and when a reading novice spells out a written or printed text, letter by letter, he hears the coherent words and phrases and can grasp their meanings. If we would apply the same method to a musical line, calling out the notes by name, we would not have music. When a musician reads a piece of notation, he never thinks of the names of the notes; he thinks of the sound only. Notation would have meaning for him, even if the notes had no names at all.

Further, the meaning of a note is determined by its relation to a larger unit, to a group of subsequent and coinciding notes. The absolute pitch of an individual note is not decisive. A given piece of notation can be transposed up or down; the notes will change, yet their relationship and consequently their musical meaning will remain the same.

Musical notation, therefore, is not alphabetical writing, but more like hieroglyphs. It is the *pictogram of the sound,* showing the relationship of successive and coinciding tones. To be familiar with notation does not simply mean to know the names of the notes, but to take in the picture of a piece of notation as a whole, to grasp its musical meaning spontaneously, as if one were actually hearing the sounds.

29

Similarly, to be familiar with the keyboard does not simply mean to recognize the keys individually, but to coordinate finger movements with music; with both its notation and sound. A pianist's finger movements are a coherent chain and, while moving his fingers on the keyboard, he does not concentrate on the keys individually.

If a beginner, trying to sight-read, relies on the *names* of notes and keys, he perpetually has to shift his eyes between the page and the keyboard and therefore picks out notes and keys one by one. This is an utterly slow, strenuous, and confusing procedure which keeps the pupil preoccupied with details. He does not grasp the intended musical meaning, and he does not visualize the notation as a total picture. His finger movements are incoherent, his playing is extremely dragging, uneven and full of errors. He must be helped by his teacher to correct his mistakes, and is required to repeat each piece until he can play it evenly and fluently.

When he repeats a piece frequently, his finger movements become connected by habit, and in this form he eventually retains them in his memory. Then, while he plays the piece, he no longer thinks of the names of notes and keys. At the same time, he no longer follows the notation, except occasionally to prompt his memory. The notation as a whole remains mute to him.

So long as a pupil clings to the names of notes and keys, he is confined to piecemeal reading, and this obstructs further development. For mastering new pieces, he depends permanently on his teacher's assistance as well as on numerous repetitions. His troubles mount with every complication in the music; his mistakes multiply and he fails to correct them despite his teacher's aid; and his playing remains uneven and slow despite endless repetitions.

30

How to break away from piecemeal reading

Among the many pupils who are taught by the traditional method there are a few who do develop beyond the elementary phase. But they succeed only because they emancipate themselves from the names of notes and keys and from the piecemeal method described.

Some learn the trick of following the sound without paying any attention to the notation. They keep their eyes permanently on the keyboard and so they have no trouble finding the right keys. These students learn to play by ear, not from the page. They develop fluent playing, but remain confined to the music they have actually heard. With all their progress, these students show a one-sided, limited development.

Only in rare cases is a beginner fortunate enough to attack his tasks competently, that is, moving his eyes along the page, grasping the musical units without clinging to details, without thinking of the names of the notes; moving his fingers according to the picture of the notation, and finding the keys by sense of touch without looking at them. Such a student acquires a command of notation and keyboard, and the road to his steady and all-around development is paved.

While these few pupils find the effective attack by themselves, others can find it only if they are helped by a teacher.

First of all, the alphabetical method ought to be dropped. Instead of learning the names of the notes and keys, a beginner must learn to direct his fingers immediately along the musical line as seen and heard. This certainly is not an easy assignment for the average beginner; it is even more difficult for him than perfecting individual pieces. At first, a piece of notation seems to be a meaningless conglomeration of notes. But this blur becomes meaningful to the beginner if a method can be found by

31

which *he hears the actual sound while he looks at the notation.* Then the notes upon the page spring to life for him.

This is what happens when a beginner is guided by his teacher's accompaniment. Relying on it, he can more easily coordinate ear, eyes, and fingers. He can follow the musical line in its unbroken continuity, and anticipate the sound during slow playing and in spite of his errors. He hears his mistakes and can correct them by ear.

Moreover, the beginner's playing, however simple and imperfect, is transformed by his teacher's accompaniment into satisfactory sound. Thus the pupil looks upon his first piano experiences as achievements, not merely as preparatory drills. Proceeding in this method, he can spare himself dull, monotonous work. On the contrary, he is constantly stimulated by playing a large variety of good music.

Sooner or later every beginner gets over his initial difficulties, and then develops his pianistic skill with increasing ease. Eventually the pupil learns to sight-read unaided.

3. TIME AND RHYTHM

Most students taught in the conventional manner have great difficulty keeping time, and there are many who never learn to play rhythmically. Does rhythmic accuracy require an unusual aptitude? No, only adequate training; and this is not obtained by the usual aids, that is, explanation of time values, rhythmical drills, or counting.

Why are the usual expedients ineffective?

1. The time value of an individual note does not, of course, determine rhythm. The rhythmical pattern of a piece of musical

notation remains unchanged if the time value of *every* note is doubled, let us say, or every note is halved. Rhythm results from the interrelation of the time values of the notes within a unified group. We grasp this interrelation spontaneously, by our sense of rhythm, not by calculation. Everybody develops a sense of rhythm, quite irrespective of musical ear, since rhythm is not necessarily bound to notes or to sounds. A piano student's inability to play rhythmically does not signify any inherent lack of rhythmical feeling; it is just that he cannot grasp the rhythmical meaning of a given piece of notation.

2. Rhythmic drills may help a student to grasp a given rhythm as such, but not to coordinate rhythm with notation. As long as a student struggles to decipher notes and to find keys, he cannot be expected to observe rhythm too. Though such a student *could* easily grasp the rhythmic pattern of a piece, he involuntarily adjusts his playing to the changing difficulties in the piece—speeding up at easier passages, slowing down at harder ones, shortening long notes and lengthening short ones.

3. He cannot improve by counting. Making a beginner count while he sight-reads imposes an additional burden upon him. If he is having trouble keeping time, he will count as unevenly as he plays. Even if his teacher counts for him, he is often unable to adjust his playing to the count.

How does a student learn to keep time?

Only those students learn to keep time by themselves who learn to play at sight by themselves. All the others can learn to keep time as they learn to play at sight, namely, by following their teachers' accompaniment.

All the pupil has to do is to strike the notes simultaneously with his teacher. For this purpose no arithmetical explanation, no drill, and no counting is necessary.

Nowhere does guided sight-reading show its effectiveness as clearly and quickly as in the problem of time and rhythm. A student who from the beginning is guided by his teacher's accompaniment hardly feels that keeping time and rhythm is a particular problem. From the time he has learned to follow his teacher, he can control his time and rhythm throughout the increasing difficulties up to the most intricate patterns. Gradually the student learns to associate his own rhythmic response with the corresponding appearance of the printed music. Then he will be able to read spontaneously any rhythm from notation, and he will become independent of his teacher's guidance.

4. FINGERING

To achieve a well-rounded performance, a piano student must play with a coherent chain of finger movements, and thus has to use proper fingering. Therefore, it seems logical to give a student detailed fingering instructions in order to help him achieve this performance. This is indeed one of the conventional principles of piano teaching, particularly elementary teaching.

Usually, however, a teacher has difficulty in carrying out this principle. Most beginners, absorbed in deciphering the notes, tend to disregard printed guides and use uncontrolled, inappropriate fingering. The teacher repeatedly calls these marks to the pupil's attention. And if the pupil does observe the marks, his finger movements do not necessarily become coherent. For a pupil who is still wrestling with notes and keys cannot control his finger movements. Many beginners, in their attempts to play from notes, are unable even to hold their hands still. If a teacher insists that a beginner observe the finger guides and achieve integrated finger movements, the pupil is forced into the conventional routine of perfecting pieces.

However, if a student, whether by himself or under a teacher's guidance, learns to grasp a group of notes as a unified whole and to anticipate the sound, he can also learn to coordinate and anticipate the impending finger movements as a coherent chain (and thus achieve well-rounded playing). It is only after he has reached this stage that the student can fit his finger movements to the printed guides, but by then his fingers have learned to find their way safely without editorial assistance.

In other words, while a student can derive well-rounded playing from fingering, the more fortunate student derives his fingering from well-rounded playing.

The first one pieces his finger movements together through mechanical repetition. In this way, all he learns is to master each of his pieces individually. This achievement does not benefit him in the learning of another piece. Moreover, his facility remains limited to rather simple music.

The other student, however, who learns to coordinate his finger movements to the picture of the notation as a whole can keep pace with the growing difficulty of his material. Through working on a large volume and variety of music, he develops a reliable and comprehensive finger sense.

Since sight-reading offers the greatest opportunity for volume, variety and developing coordination, it is the most effective training for finger sense as well. A good sight-reader indeed finds adequate fingering automatically, even when he plays a piece at first sight. If he tried to observe the printed fingering, he would be handicapped rather than helped.

Likewise, an advanced student, working to perfect a piece, depends much less on the printed finger guides than on his sense of fingering.

Unnecessary finger marks

Nevertheless, not only the conventional pieces for beginners, but also the usual editions of piano literature meant for advanced students, are lavishly supplied with finger guides, many of which appear banal and self-evident to an advanced student. Frequently, groups are marked note by note, where just one characteristic mark would suffice. When a figure is repeated, we sometimes find the fingering indicated for each repetition. Many of the marks could be replaced by others equally serviceable. Sometimes the choice is left to the student, but not entirely so, for a group of alternatives is provided. Many places are marked where fingering should be of no importance at all—at slow passages, long notes, isolated notes, etc. Often the easy sections of a piece are fingered as copiously as the difficult sections.

Much effort has been expended on crowding the pages with fingering signs, with the result that practically nobody pays any heed to them at all. If a student tried to follow faithfully all the printed marks, he would be so finger and key conscious that he would have considerable trouble holding the musical line together. Fingering should be a help, not an order, and therefore should be marked, if at all, at points only where it offers a particular advantage.

Complicated fingering

Oddly enough, many fingering guides are not at all advantageous but make the performance harder instead of easier. Some are remnants of the time when pianists used organ fingering, strictly connecting the tones and even resorting to the fussy "silent" finger changes on a key.

Most of the complicated fingering instructions found in students' editions are accomplishments of the nineteenth century, the era of the concert pianist, when technical difficulties counted more than did musical ideas. This standard of taste led to the overemphasis of fingering and to athletic mannerisms. One of the first pianists who introduced useless difficulties in hand movements, as indicated in his compositions and piano arrangements, was Liszt. Without any necessity, he often played with his left hand alone or with his hands crossed, and also in other ways many of his finger marks make the performance needlessly difficult.

Prominent among the pioneers of "modernized," that is, tricky, fingering was Hans von Bülow. He tried to adjust fingering to dynamics and phrasing, using strong fingers for loud notes, weak fingers for soft notes, staccato fingering for detached notes—this is, a fingering which would prevent the player from connecting the notes—and the like.

The peak of absurdity was reached by Hugo Reimann. He maintained that the old simple fingering which had reduced the amount of hand movement was obsolete. He pleaded for "liberty to move the hand," and devised a fingering system that perpetually kept the player's hand restless and completely occupied his mind.

Strangely enough, almost all editors for the next decades followed Bülow's and Riemann's examples. A few maintained that fingering intricacies stimulated the player's imagination and helped him improve the expression of his performance. As if music itself were not stimulating enough and expression depended on fingering!

Printed music today; at least in some editions, has returned to more reasonable fingering but still clings to one traditional mannerism, namely, making obligatory a change of fingers in repeating a note. Such a change is sensible perhaps when a note is to be repeated in very rapid succession, particularly when several repetitions follow in a row. But in the usual editions the fingers are required to change in *every* case of repetition, even of long notes, in slow tempo, when the notes are separated by rests or by other notes, as in mordants, trills, etc.

No specific examples of extravagant fingering have to be presented here, since the reader may open any page of one of the older or newer student editions and find abundant samples in every staff if not in every measure.

Fingering which a well-trained pianist finds by himself without conscious effort is rather simple. Intricacies of fingering are artificial and contradict a natural motor sense.

For the use of sight-reading exercises for the advanced student, the most instructive editions are those with no finger guides at all. These editions may also be used for repertoire study; the student is free to mark critical passages with fingering of his own choice.

Unedited reprints of original editions of piano classics have begun to appear, unadulterated by fingering or other guides. This plain notation is a blessing to the eyes of a player who looks for music rather than for technical suggestions.

5. VELOCITY

A player's fingers cannot travel faster than the thoughts which direct his fingers on the keyboard. Therefore his velocity depends first on his mental agility in grasping printed music and coordinating finger movements; second, his fingers must be agile enough to keep pace with his thoughts.

To speed up very simple figures—repetition of a note, trills, etc.—a player need have no more than agile fingers. A more complex musical structure, however, calls for quicker coordination.

According to traditional methods of instruction, the student is supposed to develop finger agility by doing "technical exercises," whereas quick coordination, it is expected, will be learned by perfecting repertoire pieces individually.

When a student plays at first sight a piece of considerable difficulty, his eyes cling to each musical unit for a while, until he has grasped its meaning and has found the corresponding finger movements. When he repeats the piece, his thoughts run faster from unit to unit and his playing gains speed.

The conventional rule has been: "Play your piece at first at a slow pace; when you feel secure enough, play it faster; keep on repeating the piece, speeding up gradually until you arrive at the intended tempo."

How does repetition work?

If speed could increase in proportion to repetition, every student would be able to master any piece simply by repeating it often enough. Yet experience has shown that only students with a quick grasp arrive at the full speed, and this after a comparatively small number of repetitions. The others have to repeat their pieces endlessly in order to increase the speed at all, and still their performance lags behind the correct tempo.

A slow pupil cannot push his playing at will. This is most clearly demonstrated if, as is sometimes recommended, he practices with a metronome. With all his effort to speed up, and in spite of arduous repetition, it becomes increasingly difficult for him to keep pace with the metronome; he grows tense, and his playing becomes uneven, replete with stumbling and blurring.

In working on a piece, a student should not try to force speed. He must play at ease throughout, and remain relaxed. Nevertheless, in the course of the repetitions, involuntarily and almost unconsciously, he gradually will increase his speed.

When we watch a student working on a piece in this way and use a metronome to measure his improvement, we find that the first repetitions help him increase his speed noticeably. Each additional repetition is less and less effective, until finally the tempo remains stationary. Subsequently, say on the next day, when the student resumes work on the same piece, he starts with a lower speed than the top speed of the day before. His second day's repetitions follow the same pattern as the day before and he arrives at a higher ultimate speed than on the first day, but again his tempo reaches a plateau. The same is true on succeeding days. The net gain in speed lessens from day to day. Eventually, further repetitions are ineffective, and the whole process comes to a standstill.

For the mathematically minded reader the process is illustrated by this graph:

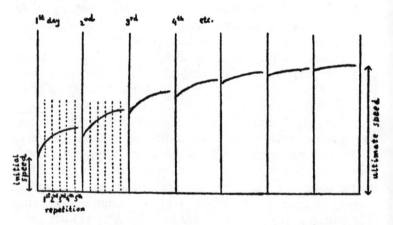

In testing a number of students of various degrees of facility, each one working on pieces of various degrees of difficulty, we found a fairly definite relation between a student's initial speed

—the speed at which he played a piece at first sight—and the ultimate speed which he could achieve by repeating the piece. On the average the first speed was multiplied four or five times. Thus a student, who can play a piece at first sight with half the necessary speed, will easily and quickly master that piece at its correct speed. If he starts at one-fourth or one-fifth of the required speed, it will take much time and a great many repetitions to perfect the piece. If his initial speed is only one-tenth of the designated speed, he will arrive at no more than half of it, no matter how diligent he may be.

Various techniques of perfecting a piece have been suggested for the slow student. The oldest method was *dissection*. The student was instructed to break the piece horizontally and vertically into small bits. He was to repeat each fraction separately, then piece them together bit by bit until he had reassembled the piece.

How does the dissecting method work?

To speed up a small group of notes is, of course, much easier than to speed up a whole piece. The student can soon play each of the small groups at full speed. But as he gradually reassembles them, his playing slows down more and more. Finally, when he arrives at the fully reassembled piece, he plays as slowly as he played it at first sight. The dissection method takes a great deal of time and does not help the student attain a higher speed.

Here is the explanation of this fact:

When a student plays an isolated fraction of a piece, he has to concentrate on this fraction only; if he plays the piece in its continuity, he must, while he plays one fraction, anticipate the next one. To play a group of notes and at the same time anticipate the next group calls for quite a different process of thought from that involved in playing groups separately.

41

When a student practices with each hand separately, the train of thought follows a horizontal path in each separate staff. Afterward, when he attempts to play the two hands together, he must integrate both parts by a thought pattern which involves vertical as well as horizontal reading. This new mental pattern, because of the added vertical component, is entirely different from the previous left and right hand pattern.

In short, the player's train of thought in directing his fingers is not merely a sum of its elements but the outcome of a synthetic mental process by which those elements are integrated into an *indivisible whole*. Therefore, the speed which is attained by practicing the parts cannot be transferred to the whole.

Today the dissection method is applied only occasionally, mainly to extremely difficult pieces or passages. Some teachers suggest practicing variants of such pieces or passages as a preparatory exercise. Yet no method is more effective than the repetition of a piece as a whole.

How is velocity developed?

When a student tackles a piece and starts out with a far too slow tempo, he must recognize that he cannot gain mastery of that piece by working on it alone, no matter how industriously. Nor is there any technique of practicing which can help raise too slow an initial speed to the correct ultimate speed. There is only one way of achieving this goal: *To increase the initial speed*. The student must learn to grasp music and musical notation more quickly and to coordinate his finger movements more quickly.

A student's grasp and coordination grow with the volume, variety, and difficulty of his study material. His skill develops as rapidly as he advances with his study material.

A student taught by conventional methods, on the other hand, advances with his study material only as rapidly as he learns to perfect his pieces. Hence it follows that an initially slow student lags more and more behind a faster one.

To make progress, a student need not work out his pieces to the point of perfection. He develops velocity by his mental effort, when he plays a piece at first sight and during the first repetitions. Additional repetitions require less and less effort and may help the student only to achieve a better mastery of the particular piece.

While a repertoire student spends all his time on one piece alone, a sight-reading student can use the same period of time for working on fifty pieces of the same degree of difficulty. He does not have to bother with the mastery of them at full speed, but during this period his initial speed on new pieces will increase noticeably. Furthermore, he will become eligible for pieces of the next degree of difficulty. Then, when he works on a larger number of harder pieces, his velocity will improve still further, so that if he now tackles an easier piece, his initial speed will be much higher than it was previously for that grade.

Sight-reading is the only effective velocity training for the slow student, because it encourages him to advance rapidly from easier to harder pieces throughout his studies. He will play very slowly for quite a while and he should do so, but his velocity will steadily increase. The lag between him and the initially quicker student will be reduced in time.

6. Finger Agility and Technical Exercises

"Technical exercises," comprising a variety of simple and monotonous figures, were devised around 1800 to equip students to meet the demands of piano literature. At that period velocity passages usually were composed of simple figures, while complex musical structure was limited to slow movements.

In later pianistic works, however, the performer had to master increasingly complex music in velocity passages. It was recognized that speed which a student had developed in simple figures cannot be transferred at will to complex compositions. Therefore, during the nineteenth century, exercises of more complex styles were published for students.

The masters of Romanticism, above all Chopin, created the concert étude, which, however, was meant for performance rather than the development of technique.

It became more and more obvious that no amount of practicing exercises and études could in itself prepare a student for the immense variety of pianistic problems presented by composers of the late nineteenth and the twentieth centuries.

Many modern teachers recognize the inadequacy of the traditional "technical exercises." They suggest that students can develop most phases of technique by working on the repertoire literature itself, and that technical exercises should be reduced to the minimum required to develop agility of hands and fingers and to keep them in good form.

The "piano hand"

Formerly it was generally believed that the anatomical peculiarities of a piano student's hands and fingers were responsible for the development of his skill. It was also believed that an anatomically inferior hand could be improved by gymnastic exercises done on the piano, or on a silent keyboard, or detached from any keyboard. Such exercises also were supposed to equalize the natural difference in velocity between the "weak fingers" —4 and 5—and the "strong fingers"—1, 2, and 3.

Many students, however, develop amazing technique in spite of small, plump, or rigid hands, and many who are endowed with typical "piano hands" remain slow. Some students develop high finger velocity, though they undergo very little finger training or none at all, while others who devote much time to such training show insufficient results. If nimbleness and strength of hands and fingers could be improved by moving them diligently, normal playing would do all that was needed. Why then should the pupil be bothered with exercises which are not only boring but which might also overstrain his muscles and sinews?

A student's finger agility depends less upon the *anatomy* of his hand than the way he *uses* them. Awkward, inappropriate positions and movements of hands and fingers do slow down the student's playing. His fingers seem to fall behind his thoughts, and he gets the sensation of "disobedient fingers." Actually, however, hands and fingers follow thoughts automatically; they need no gymnastics to obey. What the student must learn is to give his fingers the proper commands.

Planning of finger movements

Scientific-minded teachers came to the same conclusion.

They at first tried to explore the playing of proficient pianists, analyzing positions and movements, the distribution of strength and weight of the player's fingers, hands, arms, and his whole body; they even studied functions such as breathing. For a more minute investigation, slow motion pictures of professional performances were taken.

These studies did not abolish, they merely yielded new types of, technical drills: simple movements on the keyboard or away from it, planned with precision. Even beginners had to do such drills, in order to *prevent* the incorrect use of hands. These drills, persistently practiced, were supposed to establish for the student a set of mechanical habits that would function under any circumstance.

Has experience borne out these expectations? No, because though these drills may prepare a pupil to play simple figures at a high speed, they do not enable him to transfer the same velocity to a complex musical structure, where he is confronted with problems of coordination. While he is engrossed in these, his hands and fingers almost inevitably fall back into their inappropriate positions and movements.

Teachers who devise these drills can tell us *how* a player ought to move his fingers, but the critical question is *why* a player moves them as he does.

A player's movements on the keyboard are not simply "habits" which he manifests under any conditions. His movements are *symptoms,* that is, they involuntarily display the state of his mind while playing, and his attitude toward piano work. His hands speak a language as revealing as unconscious facial expression and gestures. We see this most clearly in beginners. Listless beginners play with slack, flabby movements; trembling fingers indicate fear of making mistakes; clumsy and jittery movements indicate confusion in the pupil's mind while he follows musical notation. A beginner's fluency problem is not to improve his finger movements as such, but to change his attitude toward piano work.

When we watch a beginner's awkward movements on the keyboard, we may be tempted to think, "How can he ever achieve fluency? How can he ever connect movements, each of them obstructing connection? First of all he must correct each movement!"

We have found that exactly the opposite is true: at first a student must learn to connect his movements by coordinating them to music; later he will find correct finger movements automatically.

Among advanced students, the most widespread weakness is impatience. An impatient student is accustomed to practicing at his top speed, almost on the verge of losing evenness and accuracy. He gets into a permanent state of mental tension, which is transferred to his muscles, and so the agility of his hands and fingers is thus impaired. His impatience diminishes his velocity instead of increasing it.

Also, if a student pushes his fingers, the less flexible ones—4 and 5—fall behind the others. His playing may be up to tempo, but it will not be "brilliant," as minutely equalized tempo rather than breath-taking speed is what makes for "sparkling brilliance." Equalized tempo does not depend upon physically equalized fingers, for they cannot be equalized.

Relaxation

The source of brilliance as well as of finger velocity in general is *relaxation*. Many teachers assign special relaxation drills to their students. Yet relaxation and tension are not fixed qualities. The overambitious student who tries to force his speed may well relax when he does schematical drills designed for that purpose, because they do not arouse his ambition. The moment that he is confronted with challenging music, however, he becomes tense again.

Instead of describing the relaxed movements of a good pianist, we should focus on the reason for his relaxation. He simply possesses from the outset enough patience and self-control to restrain himself and to practice with less speed than he can actually muster. As his mind is perfectly relaxed, the tension of his muscles will automatically be reduced to a minimum. His speed nevertheless increases steadily. When he eventually reaches the required speed for any piece, he will still perform it with ease and will maintain perfect control of his fingers.

In short, and oddly enough, finger velocity is developed by practicing slowly.

Finger control

Every piano pupil can control his movements on the keyboard while doing schematical exercises, since he is emotionally rather indifferent to them. It is when he is confronted with complex musical structure and notation that his reluctance, fear, confusion, impatience, or any other emotional attitude toward his piano work may be aroused and cause inappropriate finger movements.

Swimming can be learned only in water. A person who practices swimming movements on dry land does not repeat them effectively in water, for in the water an emotion, the fear of drowning, is aroused and makes him lose control of his movements.

Manual awkwardness, like any other shortcoming, can be successfully fought only at its root. Finger exercises cannot help overcome awkwardness; they can prove harmful, since they make a student finger-conscious. Specialized exercises may overstress difficulties. Many students have a definite horror of scales, of octaves, of double-thirds, or other such tasks, and stumble over them in real music, for no other reason than that they had practiced them in special exercises.

Overemphasis on technical exercises may also divert a student from expression to velocity, and thus dry out his performance.

If a student practices his pieces throughout with the working habits and in the manner described in the previous chapters, he develops a comprehensive, never-failing motor sense; and this is the basis of manual dexterity.

Finger agility, like quick coordination, is not a particular branch of piano study; it grows automatically, parallel to the student's general musical and pianistic development, without conscious finger-control and without special exercises. It is, therefore, all the more important to help a plodding pupil develop correct working habits. The most effective "exercise" to accomplish this is a program of guided sight-reading.

7. Expressive Playing

According to conventional methods, a student is introduced to the art of playing expressively by learning to observe the printed marks of expression. Yet, using this method, only few students develop expressive performance, while the playing of the others remains lifeless and "mechanical," however carefully they may follow these marks.

Colorful tone or colorful performance?

Many teachers believe that the real source of expressive playing is a particular coloring of the piano tone which can be controlled by the player's touch. They stress the difference between striking a key with the weight of the finger, the hand or the whole arm. They consider the angle between the striking finger and the key, the pressure upon a key while holding it down, the finger movement in leaving a key, and the like. They use various systems of touch regulation and assign special exercises, even to beginners, with the purpose of producing "expressive tones."

The notion of touch and tone control is so widespread that we hear about a pianist's "tone" as if he were playing the violin. He is praised for his "singing" or "sensual" or "cultivated" tone; or criticized for his "harsh" or "rough" tones.

Actually, the tone color of a piano cannot be changed, however the player may modify his touch. The tone quality is completely determined by the mechanism of the piano. The tone of the modern piano is percussive rather than expressive. It has a wide dynamic range and allows clear, brilliant playing. Older types of piano had a more colorful sound, rich in overtones; also, the tone, particularly in the higher octave registers, was more voluminous and sustained.

Yet it was not easier to achieve expressive playing on those old instruments than it is on ours today, and the problem of expression would remain even if pianos were constructed with a more colorful tone. We have all heard singers who have charming voices—or violinists who display exquisite tone—but whose performance is nothing more than a sequence of beautiful sounds, the whole uninspiring. Yet other artists can, with less than first-rate voices or tone quality, achieve superb expression.

To be sure, we can describe a piano performance as more or less colorful, but this has nothing to do with the color of a single tone in terms of acoustics. A "colorful" performance is simply an expressive one, and therefore "color" in this figurative sense can emerge only when a piece or a section of it is played as a whole, and not as a result of "touch" exercises.

The sources of expressive playing

ANALYTICAL APPROACH

A pianistic performance as a whole can be very expressive even though single piano tones lack color. The player can make up for this lack by shades of strength and timing of the tones, and also to a certain degree by use of the pedals. Modern piano music is indeed more lavishly supplied with guides for these shades, and in study editions of the classics, too, shades, in addition to those in older prints, have been indicated by editors. Some of them even go too far and suggest shades that are hardly compatible with the older styles. This is particularly true for early pieces which were written for the harpsichord; their style is marred if they are performed with modern dynamics and phrasing.

Yet, apart from the question of style and taste, overdoing nuances does not enhance performance. If a pianist is too much engrossed in details, his playing loses spontaneity. Least of all can a plodding student achieve expressiveness by laboring over shadings.

Expressive playing is an organic whole which cannot be described, calculated, or pieced together by painful attention to detail. Instead of dissecting the performance of a good pianist, we should look at it as a whole. True, a virtuoso does ponder somewhat over shadings, but he has from the start grasped the expression of the piece as a whole, and spontaneously. This attack enabled him to find the corresponding shades automatically, particularly those which are much too subtle for conscious control. Yet exactly by such shades does a pianistic performance spring to life. It is these infinitesimal shades rather than the obvious ones that reflect the player's temperament and frame of mind, his maturity and imagination, in short, his whole personality.

ROMANTIC APPROACH

Expressive playing is a matter of emotion, not of intellect. Many composers have realized the inadequacy of the conventional marks of tempo, dynamics, and phrasing; they have added other marks, indicating the mood of a piece or a section of it. Terms such as "affectionately, passionately, vigorously, cheerfully, gracefully, with longing" are to be found in Beethoven's later works. Schumann, Liszt, and other Romantic composers used such markings on an even larger scale. Still later, these markings became a mannerism. Eventually the practice subsided.

Denoting the mood helps very little to solve the problem of expressive playing. Many styles of music do not express high-strung romantic feelings, and many musical emotions have no equivalent among everyday emotions and hardly can be expressed by language. Yet even where the indication of the mood *is* adequate, it helps only those students who have already mastered expressive playing. The others may understand the mood of a composition when they listen to its performance. This, however, does not necessarily enable them to express that mood in their own playing. Many students cannot grasp the emotional content of music at all, particularly of non-romantic styles.

PSYCHOLOGICAL APPROACH

The most effective way to experience musical feelings and to express them in one's playing is to combine listening and playing. Thus a student can develop expressive playing through guided sight-reading by adjusting his playing to his teacher's accompaniment. This does not mean that he mimics the nuances note by note. What happens is that the accompaniment conveys the teacher's musical emotions; the student's own feelings are aroused, and these he expresses spontaneously in his playing without being told how. In this way, he gradually and without self-consciousness develops interpretative skill and touch control.[1] Eventually he acquires independence of expression; he learns to grasp the mood of a composition and is free to develop his own musical personality.

8. Pianistic Memory

Most students who are taught in the usual way have considerable trouble perfecting their repertoire pieces even if they practice from notes only; but their troubles are multiplied when they have to learn their pieces by heart. They must labor arduously to memorize even a short and simple piece and must repeat it by heart continuously to retain it. The memorizing process does not become easier for them if they expand their study material. With increasing complexity of material, the number of repetitions required to memorize a piece increases enormously, and soon students arrive at the limit of their memorizing capacity.

Various techniques of memorizing have been suggested to help a pupil in his struggle, such as dissecting the piece and reassembling the memorized fractions, practicing variations of a piece or its sections, analyzing the form and harmonies of the

[1] This also includes the skill to strike two or more keys with one hand simultaneously and with different strength ("polydynamics"). To manage this, various instructions have been offered, as how to hold hands and fingers, and how to distribute the weight of the hand between the striking fingers. A student who follows these instructions may succeed in striking an isolated double-note or a chord with the intended dynamic shades, but this does not enable him to manage the same chords in a coherent chain or to play several coinciding voices with one hand, stressing one of them throughout. Polydynamics cannot be learned by such instructions or drills. Neither advice nor drill is necessary if the student practices in an effective manner, that is, while he plays (and repeats) his pieces at sight, he makes for himself an accurate inner image of all the dynamic shades encountered. In the course of his practicing, his sound-images materialize spontaneously and automatically in his playing. In this way he learns to carry out all kinds of polydynamic shades, unconscious of the piano mechanics involved.

piece, copying the notation, etc. Such drills may offer a student some advantage in memorizing a piece, but with every new piece he faces the same struggle as with the first and he cannot keep pace with the growing complexity of music.

No mnemotechny or diligence will help a student who does not possess a good *pianistic memory*. But a student who does possess it has no trouble memorizing pieces of even a complex structure, and he need not resort to particular memorizing techniques.

What is pianistic memory?

Is pianistic memory based upon *motor* memory? Does a pianist, when he plays by heart, rely on the recollection, conscious or unconscious, of his finger movements? Or is pianistic memory basically *visual*? Does a pianist, in memorizing a piece, lean upon his recollection of the notation?

If one or the other were true, pianistic memory could be developed through sight-reading exercises, for these give the student a chance to experience a large number and variety of finger movements as well as notation images, and so both his finger memory and note memory would certainly be strengthened. But the fact is that among well-trained sight-readers many have great difficulty memorizing.

Apart from schematical exercises, the chains of finger movements on the keyboard are much too complex and subtle to be retained as movements in the player's memory. And even a player with a good visual memory cannot retain the notation of a somewhat complex musical notation vividly enough to rely on it. When a pianist plays a piece by heart, what he is recalling is its *sound*. If he thinks of the notation also, he is doing it only in association with the sound.[1] His fingers, however, do not follow the indirectly (and rather vaguely) recollected picture of the notation, but his recollection of the sound.

Thus, pianistic memory includes two abilities: 1) *musical memory,* namely, the ability to retain the meaning and sound of music; and 2) *the ability to coordinate finger movements with the sound.*

How is pianistic memory developed?

Musical memory is developed through the absorption of a large volume and variety of music. It follows then that sight-reading is excellent training for musical memory, but not for pianistic memory. As long as a student plays from notes, he coordinates his finger movements to the music indirectly, via the picture of the notation. For direct coordination, he must break away from this crutch. He must learn to play without notes, *by ear.*

Indeed, every player who enjoys good pianistic memory can

[1] A conductor who memorizes a score does not, as one might think, retain the picture of the notation as such. When he reads a score, he imagines its sound to its last detail. After he repeats the reading, he retains the sound image vividly. And when he conducts by heart, he associates in his mind the image of the notation with the image of the sound.

Thus, a musician's visual memory (memory for notation) appears to be the combination of his musical memory (memory for the sound) with his ability to reconstruct the notation from his recollection of the music.

Visual memory is developed through note-reading and still better through writing. A musician who is well trained in writing music can, while he hears a piece of music, imagine the notation even if he has never seen it. In an anecdote about Mozart it is related that he once listened to the performance of a work by another composer and afterward wrote down its score. This tale, apart from its exaggeration, contains nothing astonishing. To write down music which one remembers does not require the genius of a Mozart.

55

play by ear; and vice versa, a player who cannot play by ear has a poor memory.

A successful student usually starts his pianistic career by ear, picking out familiar melodies on the keyboard. Later, he tries to supply harmonies to the melodies, but since he cannot accurately retain the harmonic and polyphonic structure which he hears, he reproduces simplified versions, preserving merely the essence of the original version.

Such work involves a definite *constructive* activity which in turn helps to develop direct coordination of finger movements to music, paving the way for the ability to reconstruct music of any structure in full detail.

Every piano student can take up practicing by ear at any time. Modern progressive teachers have introduced practicing by ear and constructive work (improvisation) as additional subjects of piano study, and they have connected these with writing exercises. In writing down his improvisations and discussing them with his teacher, a student also learns musical terminology, the peculiarities of notation, and the laws of musical structure.

Constructive work not only helps the student develop pianistic memory but also gives him an intimacy with musical forms; it helps him acquire a deeper understanding of music and a quicker grasp. This in turn expedites his sight-reading facility and improves his expression in playing. Last but not least, constructive exercises encourage the student's critical attitude toward musical literature and help him develop discriminating taste.

Thus, to do constructive work appears to be worth while apart from the goal of playing by heart.

Sight-Reading versus Repertoire

To sit down and read a piece at the piano looks easy compared with working the piece out to a point of perfection. Analogously, a method based on sight-reading instead of repertoire study would seem to be superficial, especially if the sight-reading method forces the teacher for a long period to disregard the pupil's hand positions, fingering, expression, tempo—to ignore every aspect of his playing, in fact, except accuracy and evenness.

Nevertheless, as we have noted in the previous sections, sight-reading enables a pupil to make steady progress, and eventually to master the instrument as a whole, and independently.

To achieve this goal, a student merely has to have the necessary perseverance. He need not be equipped from the beginning with a particular aptitude for piano playing; he can develop this aptitude through his piano work.

Thus, sight-reading offers a chance to all students, including the less gifted, which repertoire study offers to the gifted only.

How is it possible that the seemingly superficial sight-reading method proves in the long run to be more effective than the thorough repertoire method?

Repertoire study is thorough only insofar as a student perfects individual pieces; meanwhile his general development is neglected. It is like the tactics of a leader of an army who is interested in winning battles rather than the war.

A sight-reading teacher, however, though he temporarily tolerates his student's imperfect performance, persistently pursues the other, the far more important, aim: the student's steady development. This aim is achieved mainly by three devices: rich study material; approaching pianistic tasks and problems as a whole; concentrated mental effort.

Rich study material

If, as in the conventional methods, good performance is stressed from the beginning, a student must handle individual pieces with the utmost care. He must not scatter his efforts over a large repertoire; nor is he encouraged to take chances with too hard pieces. Students are advised to "learn fewer pieces thoroughly rather than more pieces superficially," and "perform easy pieces perfectly rather than difficult pieces imperfectly." A less gifted pupil is kept working on every piece for a long period of time, and he has no access to more difficult pieces, those which he is not able to perfect.

Pianistic skill, however, is a comprehensive skill, like the command of a language or of mathematics. One cannot master a language merely by learning to recite a few poems, and one cannot become a mathematician by learning only the multiplication table. How then can we expect a piano student to acquire a mastery of the instrument merely by learning a small repertoire?

Therefore, the above-mentioned mottoes should be reversed: *Desist for a while from performance rather than reduce the study material and avoid difficulties.*

Approaching the whole

A pianistic task, namely, to render a musical composition, is a whole, and *a whole is not simply the sum of its parts.*

A melody or a harmony is more than the sum of its tones. A rhythm is more than the sum of time values. A musical form is more than a sum of melodies, harmonies, and rhythms. A piece of notations is more than the sum of its notes. A chain of finger

58

movements on the keyboard is more than the sum of its elements. And the expression of playing is more than the sum of its shades.

A whole must be grasped spontaneously; not by its parts, but *before* them.[1]

The conventional expedients of repertoire study are altogether limited to details. In the previous chapters we have seen in various specific cases that a pupil, by approaching details, is not helped but sometimes even hindered in meeting his task as a whole. Thus, we should no longer wonder why a less talented pupil has failed; rather we should wonder why a talented pupil succeeds. This, too, has been explained in the previous chapters: a talented pupil approaches his tasks spontaneously as wholes and finds the details by himself and often unconsciously.

The conventional system of rules offers too much to the talented student, as he finds the right approach by himself and can afford to neglect many of the rules. The same system offers too little to the less talented student, as it helps him to achieve only a very limited success, even if he faithfully follows the rules.

To help a less talented student effectively means to help him grasp the pianistic tasks as wholes. For this purpose he must learn sight-reading. To play a piece at first sight in its continuity, a pupil *must* grasp it as a whole. He is not helped by rules which focus on detail and make him conscious of piano mechanics. To render pieces as wholes, a student must observe a particular set of rules which, unlike those of repertoire study, are necessary for the talented as well as adequate for the less talented.[2]

1 "The whole is indivisible and prior to its parts; and the whole is determined by its aim, not by its parts" is one of the basic principles of *Individual Psychology* (Adlerian psychology). Abstract as this sentence sounds, it had the power to revolutionize the traditional concept of education and pedagogy.

2 See pages 64 and 65.

Concentrated effort

The rules of sight-reading do not require any unusual abilities. Every piano pupil, while playing from notes, can visualize whole groups of notes; everyone can have his eyes travel along the page and ahead of his fingers; everyone can form his finger movements according to the musical line and find the keys by sense of touch. Everyone can adjust his tempo to the difficulties of the piece and try to correct every mistake without delay. All these rules suggest only that the student should *try* his best, even though he is not expected to succeed immediately. He certainly will succeed eventually if he continues his attempts.

To observe these rules means to meet the challenge of the pianistic tasks; and to violate these rules means to avoid the difficulties of the tasks. Certainly, for an inexperienced student it is hard to coordinate the keys to the notes by grasping whole groups of notes and finding the keys without looking at them. Yet if he avoids these difficulties, his eyes become unstable and his playing will be uneven. If a student shrinks altogether from the effort of following the notes and finding the keys by touch, his playing becomes sluggish. If a student shuns the effort of preventing mistakes or correcting them, his playing will be sloppy and filled with errors.

If a student, who has studied repertoire and is familiar with the notation and keyboard, fails to play at sight an easy piece correctly and evenly, this indicates that he does not make the necessary effort. Thus, in sight-reading a psychological problem is mainly involved rather than a musical or technical problem. Repertoire study cannot help solve this psychological problem, for a student, when working out a piece, scatters his efforts rather than concentrates them.

A sight-reading student is helped in concentrating his effort if he is guided by his teacher's accompaniment. Ensemble work places the student in a more favorable "psychological situation," because he is interested in following the living sound rather than an abstract ideal of correct playing or verbal instructions. By adjusting his playing to the accompaniment the student automatically concentrates his effort.

A talented student solves this problem of concentrated effort on his own. Talent is not, as formerly was believed, an inborn predisposition from which the skill grows almost automatically. A skill develops through work. The talented, too, must work hard, but they are willing to do this work. Talent means ultimately to love work for itself, not working merely for its success.

How does "natural talent" develop?

A person's love of work results from his childhood education. Also it becomes obvious during his childhood. Pianistic talent, too, emerges early. Every proficient pianist started to work at the piano when he was a child, usually in his pre-school years. He owes his talent to this early self-training; he does not owe this training to his talent.

Nearly any child, having access to a piano, will go repeatedly to it and finger the keyboard. Sooner or later the child may by chance strike a sequence of a few notes in which he recognizes the beginning of a tune he knows. Then he is likely to try to pick out the whole tune. It will probably give him trouble, but if he keeps on trying, he will eventually succeed.

This is how a child prodigy starts his pianistic career. Gratified by his first success, he picks up one melody after another and later improvises simple harmonies for these tunes. Each success deepens his interest in purposeful work and leads him to

61

new and more challenging attempts. And these, in turn, help him achieve new and greater successes.

When he comes to formal instruction, he quickly becomes familiar with notation. Soon he becomes independent and develops a fluent performance. He learns his assigned pieces easily and holds them in his memory. For pupils on this level, playing from notes, by ear, from memory, and repertoire work are blended from the beginning, no matter how they are taught.

Such successful children are rarely found, because usually a child prefers planless toying on the piano to sustained effort. He does not even try to pick up a melody, or he shrinks from the difficulties of his first attempts and gives up instantly.

Building up talent by means of instruction

Since every piano pupil can find the correct attitude toward work if he practices sight-reading under his teacher's guidance, we no longer define "natural" talent as the pupil's capacity to learn, but as his capacity to learn by himself with a minimum of outside help. The "untalented" are those who cannot learn by themselves at all and need a maximum of help from their teachers.

A teacher who employs our sight-reading method does not discriminate between "fit" and "unfit" pupils; a pupil with more weaknesses simply needs more help.

To teach a less talented pupil means to teach him to work. This cannot be done merely by repertoire study. A repertoire student maintains his attitude toward work during all his studies; that is why his progress and the results appear to be determined by his initial ability. If a pupil follows the sight-reading method, his initial ability determines merely his response during his elementary period; his further progress depends upon the art of the teacher in winning the pupil's cooperation.

Both the repertoire teacher and the sight-reading teacher look at the talented student as the model, but from different angles.

The repertoire teacher looks at the playing of a talented student and tries to reconstruct it with the less talented student. But if a less talented student is to imitate the talented student's results, he must also imitate the latter's development. Precisely this development is the model of the sight-reading method. Our method intends to lead the less talented along the path which the talented find by themselves.

"Gypsy" method

The famous Hungarian and Slovak gypsies have a century-old musical tradition. This colorful folk has brought forth numerous excellent instrumentalists, notably violinists. They learn to play much as an infant learns to walk—without teaching methods, lessons, or drills. No written music is used. The youngster is merely given a small fiddle and allowed to join the gypsy band. He gets no explanations or corrections. He causes no disturbance, for his timid attempts are scarcely audible. He listens; he tries to play simultaneously what he hears, and gradually succeeds in finding the right notes and producing a good tone. Within a few years he has developed into a full-fledged member of the band with complete command of his instrument.

Are these gypsy children particularly gifted? No, almost any child could accomplish what they do. They respond to a sure and natural way of teaching. The band acts as a teacher talking to the pupil in the direct language of music. The novice, by joining the band, is immediately placed in the most helpful musical atmosphere and psychological situation; thus, from the beginning, he finds the right approach to musical activity.

The same method, which the inclusion of note-reading, has

proved its efficiency in juvenile orchestras and bands conducted by understanding leaders.

The application of this principle to piano playing is guided sight-reading.

Self-Instruction

If you have been taught by conventional methods and made satisfactory progress, then you owe your success largely to your good working habits. And if you lack facility in sight-reading, it is only because you have kept too closely to the repertoire work assigned to you; it simply did not occur to you to practice sight-reading as additional work.

You may take up sight-reading exercises at any time and without trouble, even if you have given up your previous studies, and even if you have forgotten your repertoire pieces. What you still retain is your musical ear and your familiarity with notation and keyboard. This will enable you to start and carry on a course in sight-reading, though you may be unaided by a teacher.

To practice effectively, observe the following rules:

Play the selected piece at sight with both hands and in its continuity. Before you begin, look at the first unit—phrase, measure. Then begin to play and have your eyes travel steadily along the notation, grasping the parts of both hands together, without shuttling between the two staves. While playing, try always to anticipate the sound of the units. Never let your fingers race ahead of your eyes. Do not look at the keyboard, not even at jumps, despite the risk of missing a key.

Set your tempo at an easy pace so that you have time to read the notation of every unit ahead, and so that you remain relaxed throughout and can keep control over your fingers, not stumbling or tripping. However, you should not develop dragging pace. Do not play at a rigid tempo like a metronome; adjust the tempo flexibly to the changing complexities of the piece, slowing down, though not abruptly, at difficult passages.

Try your best to avoid mistakes; yet whenever you do make a mistake or a slip, don't worry about it. A student with no experience in sight-reading can hardly play a piece without making errors, even if he tries his best. Accurate sight-reading is developed only by practice, and the first step you need to take toward accuracy is to deal correctly with your mistakes. Beware of making them worse by developing bad habits—stuttering, stammering, getting stuck, looking at the keys, and the like. Don't pass over your mistakes, but correct every one *by ear, on the spot and quickly,* without breaking the continuity of the musical line.

Don't fuss over fingering. Don't let the printed finger guides interfere with your sight-reading. When you use editions which are overladen with fingering marks, particularly with extravagant fingering suggestions that introduce unnecessary complications, disregard the printed guides altogether. If you observe the aforementioned rules you will soon find appropriate fingering spontaneously.

As for rhythm, try to grasp it from looking at the notation; do not count beats. Strike keys with both hands precisely together; don't develop the bad habit of retarding the right hand. Control your use of the pedal; use it only when necessary. Practice with an even and rather soft touch, and pay some attention to the shades of expression.

You can observe all these rules only if you start sight-reading with pieces within the range of your facility. Your facility with a well-studied repertoire piece is not a measure of your sight-reading facility. So don't feel badly if you have to begin your sight-reading exercises far below the level of difficulty which you have managed to overcome in working out individual pieces. It may prove too discouraging to start with overdifficult pieces. On the other hand, note that pieces—which are easy enough for you to play at first sight smoothly and fluently without any considerable effort—can help very little to improve your skill, nor can you learn from them how to meet a challenge. Sight-reading as an exercise in skill is effective only if challenging pieces are attempted.

The reading difficulty of a piece is measured not by the "blackness" of the page crowded with sixteenth and thirty-second notes, but by its musical complexity—rhythm, harmonies, polyphony. Problems which emerge only at a high speed are not serious difficulties in sight-reading exercises. A fugue may prove harder than fireworks in octaves.

Test your reading facility by trying a number of the pieces listed in the following reading program, starting with easy pieces and proceeding to harder ones. Should you have no sight-reading experience at all, confine yourself for a short while to elementary material, not harder than the conventional piano books for beginners.

Then you may proceed to classical pieces in their original versions. In the beginning select pieces that will offer a pleasing sound even if played slowly and without shades of dynamics and phrasing. Postpone working on pieces which stress harmony rather than melody and which require fluent tempo for any meaning at all, at the Preludes No. 1 and 2 of Bach's *"Welltempered Clavichord"* vol. 1, and the Finale of Beethoven's *Sonata* op. 27 No. 2.

Sight-reading program

The easiest classical piano style is represented by Haydn and Mozart. In the beginning a well-graded progressive order of sight-reading pieces is important; the following is suggested:

HAYDN
> *Sonatas*
>> No. 2 (E Minor) Finale
>> No. 6 (C sharp Minor) Scherzando
>> No. 11 (G Major) all movements
>> No. 15 (C Major) Finale
>> No. 17 (E Major) Menuetto and Finale
>> No. 19 (D Major) Finale

MOZART
> *Sonatas*
>> K. V. (Köchel Verzeichnis)
>> No. 280 (F Major) Finale
>> No. 281 (B flat Major) Finale
>> No. 283 (G Major) all movements
>> No. 310 (A Minor) Finale
>> No. 331 (A Major) Finale Alla Turca
>> No. 445 (C Major) all movements
> *Fantasia D Minor*, K. V. No. 397

Also a few pieces on the same level of difficulty by:

BEETHOVEN
> *Variations G Major* ("Nel cor piu non mi sento")
> *Albumblatt* ("Für Elise")
> *Bagatelles op. 33*
>> No. 3, Allegretto (F Major)
>> No. 6, Allegretto quasi Andante (D Major)
>> Sonatas op. 49 No. 1 and 2

Rondo op. 51 No. 1 (C Major)
Rondo A Major

Suggestions for the next grade of difficulty:

BACH

12 little Preludes No. 10 (Menuet Trio)
6 little Preludes No. 1, 2, 3, and 4
French Suites
No. 1 (D Minor) Menuet II
No. 2 (C Minor) Courante, Air, Menuet, Gigue
No. 3 (B Minor) Menuet I
No. 5 (G Major) Gavotte, Bourrée
No. 6 (E Major) Polonaise, Menuet

HAYDN

Sonatas
No. 2 (E Minor) 1st movement (Presto)
No. 4 (G Minor) both movements
No. 7 (D Major) 1st movement (Allegro con brio)
No. 9 (D Major) all movements
No. 10 (G Major) all movements
No. 15 (C Major) 1st movement (Allegro moderato)
No. 16 (G Major) 1st movement (Allegro con brio)
        and Finale
No. 19 (D Major) 1st movement (Allegro)
No. 20 (F Major) 1st movement (Allegro moderato)
        and Finale
Andante varié F Minor

MOZART

Sonatas
K. V. No. 280 (F Major) Adagio
No. 281 (B flat Major) 1st movement (Allegro)
No. 282 (E flat Major) all movements

68

No. 311 (D Major) all movements
No. 330 (C Major) all movements
No. 331 (A Major) Andante con variazione,
    Menuetto
No. 475 Fantasia and Sonata C Minor
No. 570 (B flat Major) all movements
No. 576 (D Major) all movements

SCHUBERT

Dances

Waltzes op. 9 No. 1, 2, 3, 4, 6, 10, 12, 14, 19
Ländlers op. 18 No. 1, 2, 3, 4, Ecossaises No. 1, 2, 3, 4
German Dances op. 33, Ecossaises
Galop op. 49
Valses sentimentales op. 50 No. 13
Hommage aux belles Viennoises op. 67 No. 1, 2, 5, 8, 10,
    12, 13
Valses nobles op. 77 No. 9, 10, 11, 12
Grätzer Galop
Ländlers op. 171 No. 1, 2, 3, 4, 5, 6
Scherzo B flat Major

Still harder pieces:

BACH

French Suites

No. 1 (D Minor) Sarabande, Menuet I
No. 2 (C Minor) Allemande
No. 3 (B Minor) Allemande, Anglaise, Gigue
No. 4 (E flat Major) Gavotte, Menuet, Air, Gigue
No. 6 (E Major) Allemande, Gavotte, Bourrée, Gigue

English Suites

No. 1 (A Major) Bourées, Gigue
No. 2 (A Minor) Prelude, Sarabande, Bourrées, Gigue

No. 3 (G Minor) Prelude, Sarabande, Gavottes, Gigue
No. 4 (F Major) Menuets, Gigue
No. 5 (E Minor) Prelude, Sarabande, Passepieds, Gigue
No. 6 (D Minor) Gavottes

BEETHOVEN

Bagatelles op. 33
No. 1 (E flat Major)
No. 4 (A Major)
Bagatelles op. 119
No. 1 (G Minor)
No. 3 (D Major)
No. 4 (A Major)
No. 11 (B flat Major)
Rondo op. 51 No. 2 (G Major)
Sonatas
op. 2 No. 1 (F Minor)
op. 10 No. 1 (C Minor)
op. 10 No. 2 (F Major)
op. 14 No. 1 (E Major)

CHOPIN

Waltzes
op. 34 No. 2 (A Minor)
op. 64 No. 1 (D flat Major)
op. 64 No. 2 (C sharp Minor)
op. 69 No. 1 (A flat Major)
op. 69 No. 2 (B Minor)
op. 70 No. 2 (A flat Major)
Mazurkas
op. 7 No. 1 (B flat Major), No. 2 (A minor)
op. 17 No. 1 (B flat Major), No. 2 (E Minor)
op. 24 No. 1 (G Minor)
op. 67 No. 1 (G Major), No. 2 (G Major)
op. 67 No. 3 (C Major), No. 4 (A Minor)

70

op. 68 No. 1 (C Major), No. 2 (A Minor)
op. 68 No. 3 (F Major)

MENDELSSOHN
Songs Without Words
op. 19 No. 2 (A Minor), No. 3 (A Major)
op. 19 No. 6 (G Minor)
op. 30 No. 3 (E Major), No. 6 (F sharp Minor)
op. 38 No. 2 (C Minor), No. 5 (A Minor)

After you have worked on these pieces you will have no trouble sight-reading other works by Bach (*Partitas, Inventions, Welltempered Clavichord,* etc.) as well as other masters of the harpsichord (Handel, Scarlatti, etc.), other pieces by Haydn and Mozart, and more sonatas and pieces by Beethoven, Schubert, Mendelssohn, and Chopin. The sequence of your selection will not matter much.

Finally you will have access to any piece—the harder works of the aforementioned masters as well as others (Weber, Schumann, Brahms, etc.) up to the contemporary piano composition.

In addition to piano music, the recommended sight-reading program also includes piano arrangements of other kinds of music—orchestral and chamber music, vocal, operatic and sacred music. After you have developed considerable sight-reading facility, use any opportunity for any kind of ensemble playing—duets on one or two pianos, accompaniment, and chamber music.

The main objective of sight-reading is to become familiar with the master works of music through your own playing, to appreciate them and to enjoy them. The development of your facility is but the means to reach that goal rather than an end in itself. Therefore your practicing should be a pleasure, not a duty. Select the pieces which appeal to your understanding and taste, and discard others that fail to do so.

71

For the rest, practice systematically, observing the following rules:

Repeat each piece only a few times in succession—shorter pieces perhaps three to four times, longer ones twice. You may repeat a piece on several consecutive days, then you may leave it for a time, no matter what degree of perfection you have attained. Work on several pieces, varied in style, at the same time.

This kind of sight-reading is stimulating; you hardly feel the passing of time. Don't make a session so long that you lose concentration and interest. Don't force yourself to practice at a time when you don't feel like it. You cannot force progress by overzealous effort; development takes time. An average of one hour's practice daily, well used, is sufficient to score rather rapid progress. Even a shorter study period may do so. Intervals away from the piano don't impair the learning process; once you are on the right track, your skill keeps growing even during a period of non-practicing.

Keep a record of your practicing. List the pieces you play in a chronological as well as a classified order. Jot down your remarks about each piece—how it appeals to you, difficulties, and so on. Compare these experiences with your later ones, when you will resume work on the same pieces. This will show you an interesting picture of the development of your facility, your understanding, and your taste.

It is a particular advantage of sight-reading exercises that, unlike repertoire study and technical exercises, they hardly annoy the neighbors, musical or unmusical.

In the beginning, sight-reading is a rather strenuous job, but with growing experience you will gain security and ease, your playing will become more and more colorful and fluent, and eventually your practicing hour will be a source of sheer enjoyment.

Repertoire Study

Once a young musician asked Mozart for advice on how to write a symphony. Mozart advised him against this enterprise because the musician was too young.

"But when you started writing symphonies, you were still younger," exclaimed the young man.

"I did not ask for advice," Mozart retorted.

Though repertoire study is certainly not on the level of creative work, it, too, requires maturity.

Most of the conventional rules on how to perfect a piece rest upon experience with students who were not adequately prepared for this kind of work. A student is ready to perfect a piece only if he can play it at first sight correctly, evenly, fluently, and expressively. Then he has only a comparatively short step to take to reach perfection. Working on an individual piece is not the best way for a student to transform a faulty, uneven, dragging, and expressionless rendering into a perfect one.

A student should develop all the qualities of good performance *before* he undertakes to perfect a piece. Otherwise he will face toil and trouble, and with no other achievement than the partial concealment of his weaknesses.

This especially holds for pupils who still have elementary reading difficulties. For years and years, legions of beginners have been tortured with working pieces up to the point of perfection. Often, a teacher has to labor with a pupil on every detail of a piece. The pupil, working on his pieces at home without supervision, usually produces a distorted rendition of the piece, and then the teacher has to make corrections. The pupil has to repeat a piece endlessly in order to achieve fluency, and has to go over his pieces continuously to retain them. Often enough all this drudgery is futile, as the pupil fails the moment he is required to display his skill to an audience.

There is no sound reason for starting repertoire work with a beginner. Still wrestling with initial difficulties, he hardly feels like performing for others. Nor is it advisable from an educational viewpoint for a beginner to concentrate on his playing rather than on the music. He should spend his time and effort learning to read at sight and thus to develop his general musical and pianistic facilities, rather than on building a repertoire. Then he will be spared unnecessary bother and boredom, disappointment and discouragement, competition with the talented, a feeling of inadequacy and the fear of failure.

In due time, sight-reading exercises yield a repertoire without requiring much extra work. And if the student, in addition to sight-reading, practices by ear and does constructive work, he can learn to perform much of his repertoire by heart.

Our sight-reading program includes among others the standard pieces in a pianist's repertoire. The sight-reading student should repeat these pieces periodically. On each repetition, because of his general progress, he will play a piece with greater ease and mastery than he did before. Eventually he will arrive at the point where he can easily and quickly give that piece the finishing touches required for perfect performance.

For the rest, a student should choose for his repertoire only pieces which he can master easily. While challenging material is imperative for sight-reading exercises, repertoire study should not be burdened with undue difficulties. Otherwise the student has a hard struggle for the purely technical mastery of his tasks; his musical emotions are stifled by a feeling of tension and insecurity, and the result is a dry performance.

On this point we fully agree with the teachers of our grandparents. To be sure, the well-meaning advice to avoid too hard pieces was good solely for the gifted students, since the others had trouble in perfecting any piece. Apart from technical exercises, the student's progress depended exclusively upon his repertoire work; therefore, every piece he had to perfect was about the most difficult he had ever dealt with. To meet this challenge, the traditional, fussy practicing routine was worked out.

A student who practices sight-reading has little trouble in perfecting pieces considerably easier than the sight-reading material on which he is working at the time. And with increasingly difficult sight-reading material, he is able to perfect more difficult pieces.

If a student works on a piece for which he is sufficiently prepared, he can easily bring his performance to a point of perfection by observing the following simple rules:

At first repeat the piece as a whole. Afterward you may work separately on the more difficult sections, but these sections must be integrated musical units. Don't break up a unit, don't pick out difficult passages ("bottlenecks"). Refrain from isolating the parts of each hand in difficult passages.

This also holds when you memorize a piece. Build up a repertoire by heart only after you have developed efficient pianistic memory, and select only pieces within the range of your memorizing facility.

To memorize a piece, repeat it in several sessions from notes until you can recall the music. Then continue to repeat it by heart. Keep the page open before you and glance at it whenever you get stuck. Eventually you will not need it at all.

Never look at your hands; look away or close your eyes.

Whether you practice from notes or from memory, play at all times with less speed than you actually can muster. Play with perfect ease, maintaining accuracy, evenness, relaxation, and finger control. Do not force speed when you repeat a piece; wait until you attain the indicated speed automatically.

Slow tempo is particularly important when you memorize a

piece. The more slowly you play, the more your memory is challenged and the more easily you will discover the weak spots in your performance.

Also, maintain the chosen shades of expression during all your repetitions. Your expression cannot be separated from the other qualities in your playing. Expression is not like a varnish on the surface of performance, but is interwoven with it. Should you work out a piece just technically at first, or memorize it, and try afterward to introduce shades of expression, you will face technical or memorizing troubles again, and you may also impair the expression of your playing.

Repeat each piece, or section of it, only a few times in succession. Stop the moment you feel tired or bored. Resume the repetitions the following day. "Digest" what you have learned in a session and make the intervals between practice sessions ever longer. Work on several pieces simultaneously, if your time allows it.

This kind of repertoire work offers you utmost gratification and reduces practicing hours and the number of repetitions to a minimum. Once you have learned a piece, you will retain it for a period of time even without repetitions, and after a longer interval you can brush it up quickly. Thus, you can expand your repertoire to any limit.

Suggestions for the Teacher

Our sight-reading method easily attracts students, especially those who have failed to learn by the conventional methods and who hope for a new start. It is far more difficult, however, to win *teachers* to a method which differs in almost every respect from their own training and practice. Also, a teacher who stresses performance can hardly be expected to endorse a type of exercise which, even though temporarily, neglects the requirements of good performance.

A teacher who accepts only those students of outstanding talent destined for a professional career can be interested but theoretically in our aim and method. He is engrossed in purely artistic problems, and relies on his students to develop musical and technical capacities by themselves. Only a teacher who has to deal with less talented pupils meets real teaching difficulties. Many of these teachers will likely be ready to accept one or another of the ideas presented here, and many may even have worked along similar lines before. Yet they certainly have achieved good results with conventional expedients too, and so they may wonder how to reconcile both concepts.

Now, our sight-reading method includes repertoire study, though as an optional subject and for advanced students only. The chief difference of opinion is on the question of whether a piano pupil ought to work out individual pieces in his elementary period. This question, of course, concerns solely less gifted beginners.

To combine both methods means to assign *every* pupil sight-reading exercises as well as repertoire study from the beginning. And this means, from our viewpoint, that the less gifted pupil is to develop a facility that prepares him for repertoire work, and at the same time to work on repertoire without yet being prepared for it.

To be sure, a repertoire teacher will have quite a different point of view as he cannot believe that sight-reading facility is the basis of successful repertoire study. Only a sight-reading teacher has this confidence. However, any teacher is free to gather data on sight-reading from his own experience before he forms a final judgement.[1]

Our recommendation to teachers who want to test this sight-reading method is: keep your usual routine and just add sight-reading as a new subject.

But be careful to separate sight-reading completely from repertoire study. Sight-reading is to be taught according to the following rules, unadulterated by any of the conventional devices employed in repertoire study. Only then can your students attain the goal of sight-reading exercises, and you a valid opinion of that method.

These rules are based upon wide experience. Revolutionary as they may appear to you, they will lose their strangeness with your growing teaching experience, and eventually you will find them quite natural and self-evident. This is the report of all teachers who were rather skeptical in the beginning and who for a while made only partial use of sight-reading. Yet more and more they were convinced of its efficiency until they were ready to adopt it as their fundamental method.

[1] In the beginning, the method spread very slowly and received attention from students rather than teachers. Only later, when results became apparent, did teachers increasingly adopt our method. At the same time, however, opposition developed. Some opponents tried to discredit the sight-reading method. They admitted that our students developed remarkable sight-reading facility, but maintained that our students' development was frustrated in other respects. They insisted that sight-reading exercises suppressed a student's desire and ability to perfect individual pieces and to develop playing of artistic quality.

In order to prove that such a fear was unfounded, our teachers' group arranged annual public recitals. Once a music critic reported in a music magazine: "I don't see any reason to oppose this group of teachers. Their pupils play as well as any others, and this recital differed in no wise from any other pupil's recital."

The gentleman was not prejudiced, as he was altogether uninterested in teaching. What he judged was our pupils' performance, not its background. Actually, there was indeed an essential difference between our pupils' recital and others: our program was decided only two weeks in advance; this was the time allowed our pupils—and none of them was particularly gifted—to work out the pieces assigned to them for the recital.

78

1. GUIDING YOUR STUDENT

In guiding your student, playing at the same or an adjacent piano, you are more than his instructor, for sight-reading cannot be taught by verbal instruction; rather, you are a living participant, thinking, feeling, and acting with each of your students individually. Guidance is a particular art and is best developed by working with numerous students of all types.

To guide a student correctly, you must understand him thoroughly. You can diagnose his peculiarities—and simultaneously the quality of your guidance—by analyzing his response. A student who is incorrectly guided may not respond at all or he may even become confused and play worse than he would alone.

Therefore, in order to avoid a battle on two fronts, start your training as a guide with students who, though they lack experience in sight-reading, do not have too much trouble following your playing. Pick your best students—mature, cooperative persons with some pianistic facility and good working habits.

The easiest and most effective guidance for a somewhat advanced student is at a second piano, placed so that you can watch your student. Use a duplicate music book and play in unison with him. If only one piano is available, you may use duets, alternately playing the treble and bass of each piece. Unfortunately, in the usual four-hand editions both parts are printed on different pages instead of continuously as a full score. Therefore you must be perfectly familiar with both parts in order to follow, by ear, your student's playing. When you play solo pieces with him on the same piano, you may play the treble along with him in a higher octave, while he plays the piece as a whole. Or, you may divide the piece between him and yourself, alternately playing the parts of each hand.

Select pieces which challenge your student but are not beyond his reading ability.

79

When you play with your student, listen to his playing with all the alertness and suppleness of an accompanist, but at the same time be sure to take the lead. Play each piece in its continuity and at a rather slow tempo, so that the student can follow without becoming tense. Stress the rhythm, but without exaggeration; keep the tempo even, but not too rigid. Slow down, though not abruptly, for more difficult passages whenever necessary.

With respect to dynamics also, adjust·your accompaniment to the needs of your student. Stress passages, parts, or phrases to offer him support wherever necessary; conversely, subdue or reduce your accompaniment when he leans too much on it. During slow playing, you may make it fuller in order to produce a better total effect.

You can hear each other better if both of you play rather softly. But it is important for you to play with good expression, so that your student hears a satisfactory whole, and gets the thrill of participating in the achievement.

Advise your student in the rules of sight-reading. His eyes should remain fixed on the notation and should always be a little ahead of his finger movements, so that he can anticipate both the sound and the impending finger movements; he should find the keys by sense of touch, never looking down, not even when he feels insecure or misses a key.[1]

The first objective in guided sight-reading is to accustom the student to keep ensemble discipline like an orchestra musician, observing the supreme law of subordinating himself to the total

[1] Likewise, a typist can type fluently only if he finds the keys by sense of touch. To develop this facility, the apprentice practices on a typewriter with blank keys and he locates them by looking at a chart of the keyboard.

For playing the piano, however, no such forcible device can be used to expedite the student's development. If an inexperienced student is assigned to play while the keyboard and his hands are covered, he will become completely confused. A piano student has to muster his will-power to resist the temptation to look down.

sound, never upsetting it. Urge your student to listen intently to your accompaniment throughout; he must not drown it out with loud playing or excessive use of the pedal. He has to keep pace with your playing, never race ahead of it nor trail behind it; he must not play on when you stop, nor stop while you play on. He must not drag his tempo unduly when he has trouble deciphering the notes or finding the keys; he overcomes these difficulties best by leaning on your accompaniment and combining reading with listening.

Avoid commenting on his fingering, hand position, or finger movements. Do not try to prevent him from making mistakes by warning him in advance; nor reproach him for his mistakes afterward. An ambitious student, with high standards of perfection, may even need your assurance that mistakes are nothing to worry about. Mistakes, properly identified and corrected, are a constructive step in the learning process. Perfect accuracy is not the prerequisite but the goal of practicing. Occasionally you may even pass over a minor slip in order to keep an unbroken musical line.

Use your accompaniment also to help your student deal with his mistakes. Whenever he misses a note or loses the rhythm, without being aware of it, signal him by stopping your accompaniment. He should correct the error as quickly as possible and immediately play on. Wait until he has made the correction. If he fails to help himself, repeat the correct note on your piano. He has to learn to follow this help by ear.

If a mistake confuses your student, you may repeat the whole phrase, but do not start all over again. Don't allow him to ignore his mistakes or develop other bad habits in dealing with mistakes, such as repeating the wrong note, stopping entirely, looking at the keyboard, going back at random to repeat a section. Don't let him deviate from your accompaniment in any way.

So far as possible, utter your suggestions and corrections by musical sounds rather than by words; this will hold your student to the paramount task, that of listening to your guidance. However, verbal reminders such as, "Listen to my playing, hear the whole phrase, keep going, look ahead," and others are helpful until full cooperation is established.

If the student has been trying his best to follow your guidance during his first reading of a piece, the result will show when you repeat the piece with him. He will be more at ease, play more smoothly and with fewer errors. Repeat a piece with him not more than two or three times; then proceed to the next piece.

When you continue working in this way with your students, you will learn to recognize quickly the capacities of any one student. You will find yourself anticipating his reactions from note to note, and thus be able to keep the situation under perfect control. You will also notice that he adjusts himself with increasing success to your leading. After a while he will be able to sight-read correctly by himself, and then the main purpose of your guidance will have been achieved.

2. New Students and Problem Students

Approach with particular care and tact a new student who has studied piano before. Do not subject him to much questioning or testing. Don't have him play pieces which he has studied before, unless he offers to play them. Performance of such pieces will not give you a reliable clue; only the way he tackles a new piece will do so.

You can test the student's reading ability by assigning him a few short pieces of increasing difficulty, without giving him any directions. Most students, when sight-reading by themselves, play too fast and do not follow the warning to slow down. Many approach the task very awkwardly and become confused. At any rate, make these tests short. Timid students, as well as those who never have tried sight-reading before, might be spared solo attempts altogether. Start playing with such a student at sight, using rather easy material. His response will show you his musical and pianistic background and—what is still more important—his working habits and degree of cooperation.

A student who is inexperienced in ensemble playing, or has had unpleasant experiences with it, may at first show signs of nervousness and reluctance, and his playing will not be up to his actual ability. For a while you might do well to follow his playing rather than have him follow your lead. Refrain from criticism as far as possible, encourage him, and calm him down by playing with him, select a variety of stimulating music which distracts his attention from his own playing. Soon he will accustom himself to ensemble playing, and overcome any inhibition.

Some students who have worked only on repertoire show an unbalanced, one-sided development. One can manage pieces in simple keys only; another has tremendous difficulty keeping time and rhythm. A third shrinks from contrapuntal structure. And so on. Some students are poor note-readers, but play well by ear. They have studied their repertoire pieces mainly by heart, can locate the keys only by looking at them; and therefore they cannot keep their eyes on the page or visualize the notation in its continuity. Once in a while you may meet a student who can grasp music and its notation in a trice, but is unable to follow with his fingers.

Sight-reading exercises soon help a student fill the gaps in his earlier training.

There are many students who, notwithstanding their repertoire study, have no preparation for sight-reading at all. They have no command of either notation or keyboard, they miss notes and keys throughout and cannot correct their mistakes. These students are therefore unable to follow your accompaniment, no matter how much you may slow it down. Regardless of what they have accomplished in their repertoire study, they should be hándled like beginners in respect to sight-reading.

Of the students who do have an adequate background, some may have trouble in adjusting to your guidance. They may consider your accompaniment a burden or coercion rather than a help. One may be dissatisfied with reading imperfectly and slowly; while another may be bewildered by the greater mental effort which sight-reading exacts. A successful repertoire student, however, soon adapts himself to the new method.

You can save time and trouble if you start guiding a pupil on a second piano. Some who are unable to follow your accompaniment on the same piano may respond immediately when they hear left and right hand parts together and in the original octave register. The satisfaction in using two pianos—the second one need not be a precious instrument—will more than compensate for the cost. In taking up sight-reading with students who have ineffective working habits, guidance on a second piano is almost imperative.

A student's preliminary training in repertoire is certainly an asset in sight-reading, but only if he had adequate working habits. Poorly trained students tend to follow their habits rather than your guidance. Adjustment to your guidance means an all-around readjustment as well.

In order to help such a student you have to recognize his particular bad habits. Every student has his own group of shortcomings, yet the main types turn up over and again; your growing experience in dealing with students will enable you to recognize each type immediately.

There are, for example, many students who adjust their tempo to the easy passages of a piece and keep it throughout. At harder passages they blur phrases, drop notes, and pass over mistakes. Obviously these students are mainly interested in fluency and care little for accuracy.

Other hasty students, who *also* want to play correctly, develop an uneven, bumpy playing, reflecting note by note the changing difficulties of the piece.

Some pupils have the ambition to sight-read without making a single mistake. They hesitate from note to note, look at the keys in order to be sure to hit the right one. They develop playing that drags, is filled with stops, distorts time and rhythm—equivalent to spelling rather than real reading.

A student who is anxious to avoid mistakes and to achieve fluency sight-reads in a state of tension. He easily loses control when he commits an error; he gets jittery or may be so upset that he stops entirely.

Students who shun any increased effort play much too slowly, and correct their mistakes sluggishly, if at all.

In these and other cases you may discuss your student's problems with him, if he is mature enough to understand them. However, don't expect immediate results from such discussions; habits are usually too strong to be changed merely by self-understanding. Rather counteract the student's bad habits by your guidance.

By modifying your accompaniment you can control your student's tempo. When you slow down, the impatient and hasty students are curbed and have sufficient time to follow the notation attentively, and to prepare every touch carefully. Overcautious and inert students are pushed forward when you speed up and leave them no time to dawdle or look at the keys. Your accompaniment calms a nervous student. When a student commits an error, you can regulate your playing so that, in order to keep up, he must make the correction properly.

Yet you will meet also many students who, in their first attempts, show very little response to your accompaniment. They hardly listen to it, and at difficult passages disregard it altogether. Such a student may drown your playing; he is ahead of it or lags behind it. He fails to correct his mistakes even when you stop, or he may stop while you play on. He deals with his mistakes in his own way, without leaning on your accompaniment. He does not improve by repeating a piece, guided or unguided, nor by expanding his sight-reading material.

Remember that the usual methods of perfecting a piece are ineffective for sight-reading. Do not use drills. Do not mark a student's errors in the notation or allow him to attack them by frequent repetitions of a piece or its hard sections. All you can achieve by such expedients is that the student may improve his performance of individual pieces, but this will not lead him to better working habits. Nor should he be confined to reading material easy enough to play smoothly and correctly; for then he will not make any progress at all.

Your sole task is to win your student's cooperation. You cannot help him by explanations or demonstrations; it is not understanding he lacks. It is useless to admonish him incessantly and warn him of the consequences of his incorrect working habits, since he does not lack good will either. He simply cannot control his habits. His fear and shyness of difficulties are deeply rooted, and even if, reminded by you or himself, he now and then pulls himself together, he soon relapses.

Oddly enough, you will observe that such a headstrong student may refuse to sight-read alone, but is quite willing to do it with you, though he has not yet adjusted his playing to yours. Apparently your accompaniment gives him a feeling of support, and soon it becomes evident that he does not ignore it entirely. Your guidance is not completely ineffective. It is just at first very slow to influence the student, like the constant drip of water which only in time gives evidence of having eroded a stone.

Do not expect a problem student to improve quickly. Adjustment and readjustment are slow processes. Meanwhile put up with your student's habits, however annoying they may be. Don't be afraid that his attitude will become fixed if you don't fight it with all your energy. Sooner or later your student will learn to follow your accompaniment, and then he will improve in every respect.

As varied as the problems of students appear to be, there is only one way to solve them: *Keep the students working*. Faulty playing is even more distressing to them than to you. Most weak students are always on the verge of giving up. To prevent this is your first objective. Do not reproach your student for his weaknesses; criticize him in a friendly, helpful way, never growing harsh or derogatory. Do not compare him with more successful students and avoid anything that may shake his self-confidence. Do not play his pieces to him unasked; he does not learn anything by your playing and may rather become conscious of his inadequacy—"I'll never be able to play it like *that!*"

Yet with all your indulgence never lose sight of your ultimate goal to keep the student working. Find the happy medium between tyranny and coddling. If you are too strict, he will become obstinate; if you are too lenient, he will make no progress. In either case he will give up.

To be sure, such a failure can happen at any time, but the decision to quit must be left to the student. Never suggest to a student that he give up, hopeless as he may appear. As long as he is willing to work with you, he is entitled to your help, just as a sick person is entitled to medical care so long as he still breathes.

87

If, for a time, a student fails to show any considerable progress, search for a remedy. Take responsibility for his progress. A teacher who complains over a student's shortcomings is like a physician who complains about a patient's weak constitution. It is the *teacher's* task to help his student overcome his weaknesses; this requires keen observation and ingenuity.

You must feel able to meet this task. If you are skeptical, you cannot treat your student with the necessary patience, benevolence, and good humor. He will sense your lack of faith and will become discouraged. If, however, you believe in the unlimited possibilities of instruction, you will be as interested in the less responsive students as in the more responsive. Your confidence will be conveyed to your student and he will try his best to cooperate with you. He will be rewarded with a little progress which, in turn, will strengthen his confidence. The vicious circle of his non-cooperation and failure will have been broken.

3. ELEMENTARY INSTRUCTION

The first objective of sight-reading is to develop the pupil's facility to a point where, unaided, he can correctly, smoothly, and at moderate speed play at sight or after a few repetitions any music of not unusual complexity. After this goal is reached, the teacher may also help the student develop the qualities of artistic performance.

The duration of this elementary stage is determined by the peculiarities of the pupil, the development of his musical ear, quickness of mind, maturity, interest, zeal, cooperation, available practicing time, etc. The average pupil's elementary development takes a number of years. Yet a pupil who follows our sight-reading method need not be troubled over the delay in achievement. His piano work is directed not only to a distant goal—artistic performance—but also to a goal very close to him, that is to learn and enjoy music by playing it, even though not perfectly.

In order to teach elementary sight-reading successfully, a teacher must be a well-trained musician and pianist possessing as well the necessary psychological and educational qualifications. He should meet a beginner with the same interest as he meets an advanced student. Elementary instruction deserves the same esteem as artistic instruction.

Melody

A beginner must be able to grasp simple melodies when he hears them or when they are sung with him. He needs no other prerequisites in order to play such a melody from notes, under your guidance. Start with a tune in a limited range and have your pupil play it with his right hand. Explain to him how to follow the musical line with eyes and fingers. Show him where to place his fingers and where to start. Play the tune, along with him, an octave lower and add simple harmonies.

A responsive beginner can follow if you accompany him on a second piano. With a less responsive beginner it is better to stay at the same piano during the time he plays with one hand alone, in order to give him help whenever necessary, perhaps when he loses his place in the notation or when he cannot find a key. He may follow the notation better when, while he sight-reads, you point at the notes.

He is not helped, however, if you mention the *names* of keys, notes, or intervals. Don't have him memorize them, don't write them down on the page, and don't have him use note finders, key finders, chord finders, or similar devices. Through sight-reading under your guidance, the beginner will learn to coordinate the keys to the respective notes in both clefs without knowing the names. He will learn technical terms much more easily after he has become familiar with the appearance of notation through sight-reading. Then mention the names occasionally, perhaps at the opening of a piece and in announcing the student's mistakes.

Similarly, explain time values to a pupil only after he has learned to keep time and rhythm.

To read the notes and find the keys is a difficult task. Most beginners become engrossed in details and lose the continuity of the musical line. A pupil requires a great deal of practice to grasp a unit of notation as a whole and coordinate his finger movements to it.

These difficulties are not *produced* by our method. Guided sight-reading merely brings to light all at once the initial difficulties of piano study. They cannot be eliminated by any method whatsoever, and postponement has proved ineffective. A method which protects the beginner from initial difficulties keeps him from making progress. Initial difficulties must be overcome in the beginning. Otherwise they will pile up higher and higher and become insurmountable.

The initial difficulty of sight-reading is an asset, not a liability. Therefore, put up with a beginner's response. His plodding, stammering, or otherwise faulty playing are no cause for alarm. Do not fight his weaknesses by resorting to the usual expedients adopted in repertoire teaching. All our skills develop from awkward attempts. Think of the way a little child learns to talk, to read, to write. Not long ago youngsters in school were made to repeat every word and sentence until they could read and write them correctly and fluently. Today's teaching methods favor the pupil's natural development.

Bass parts

From the beginning your pupil should sight-read parts for the left hand as well as for the right, starting with simple figures. As he will not have been taught to rely on the names of notes, he will run no risk of confusing treble with bass. Play the isolated bass parts an octave higher, along with him. Repeat the piece with him, this time playing the full piece. Should he be confused by the melody, stress the bass in your accompaniment.

Soon your pupil will learn to blend the bass into the total sound; this accomplishment is an important step in the development of his musical ear.

Fingering and hand positions

Fingering should be marked sparingly. In very easy pieces— melodies in a narrow range and simple bass figures—marks rarely are necessary. Otherwise the fingering should be marked at critical points only, perhaps at the beginning of a musical line and when the hand position changes. Whenever your pupil, while sight-reading under your guidance or supervision, interrupts himself, you may indicate the fingering to him orally.

Only a responsive beginner carries out the printed fingering. Others neglect it entirely, but some may observe it when you remind them. If a student does not respond to your admonition, do not bother him any longer; wait until he will have overcome initial reading difficulties. Pupils improve their fingering by themselves in the course of their practicing.

Appropriate hand positions likewise are to be expected of responsive beginners only. For the rest tolerate a beginner's hand positions, clumsy as they may be. To fight them is futile and needless as well. A pupil's inadequate hand positions and finger movements indicate his ineffective attitude toward work. When you, by your guidance, will succeed in changing your pupil's attitude, he will, without verbal instruction and unconsciously, improve his hand positions and finger movements.

Touch and expression

As long as a pupil is absorbed in the task of reading the notes and finding the keys, he can rarely control his touch. One student pounds the keys, another barely presses them down, still another has a touch that is unpredictable from note to note. Such pupils can observe the shades of dynamics and phrasings only by perfecting individual pieces, not while they read at sight.

Before developing habitual expressive playing, a pupil must learn to play in a relaxed, unadorned manner. This he will learn through systematic sight-reading under your guidance. You can supply him with study material that sounds tolerably well without shading. Advise him to listen carefully to your accompaniment throughout, and never to drown you out. Play your part expressively of course; this will sharpen your pupil's sensitivity and prepare him for his own expressive playing.

Sharps and flats

From the beginning every pupil should learn to play in the various major and minor keys. If he is confined to easy keys for any length of time, he will encounter much trouble when he attempts to master the more difficult ones.

Most beginners prefer the white keys and make errors when they are confronted with signatures and accidentals. These errors cannot be avoided at first, and it is futile to have the beginner memorize the signatures, or practice scales or drills for this purpose. Nor is it advisable to warn a pupil of black keys by indicating them on the page or announcing them to him in advance while he plays. Ease with signatures and accidentals comes only by trial and error in the course of reading at sight a wide variety of music in all keys. Let your pupil make mistakes, and have him correct them by ear. Eventually he will find himself at home in all keys.

Chords

After the student has had some experience in reading parts with single notes, he may proceed to double notes and chords. Advise him to look at the notation of a chord as a unit, by noting its characteristic shape, rather than try to decipher it by picking out its components individually. He should lean upon your accompaniment and try to find the chord by ear. To help him overcome the initial difficulties, you can break the chords in your accompaniment.

Jumps

From the beginning, a pupil should find the keys by his sense of touch. When jumping over a large interval, too, he should discipline himself to find the right keys without looking down at them, for his eyes must remain on the page. His hands should jump rather than tap and fumble along the keyboard. If he hits the wrong key, he should find the correct one by ear, and then go on. Eventually he will develop the feel of interval all over the keyboard.

Playing with both hands

The transition from sight-reading with one hand to sight-reading with two hands is the most critical step in the development of facility even in a responsive beginner.

Teachers have hitherto attempted to reduce the initial difficulties of two-hand playing. In former times the pupil for a long while had to play with both hands in octaves, which, however, did not enrich the music. Then he was confined to pieces with very simple and monotonous accompaniments and therefore developed a lower degree of skill in the left hand. It is very difficult to correct this deficiency afterward—least effectively through mechanical exercises for the left hand. To a student trained in such a lopsided way, contrapuntal music especially becomes a horror.

Contemporary material for beginners tends to distribute difficulties equally between the two hands, but on the whole it still lacks adequate variety of combinations: 1) the right and left hands alternate; 2) only one carries a continuous musical line while the other hand is limited to a few sparse notes; 3) a melodic line is distributed between the hands so that the picture of the notation is broken, and this causes unnecessary reading difficulties.

Instead of assigning inadequate two-hand material, extend the student's ability to read with one hand, right as well as left, until he can manage moderately complex music. Then he will be sufficiently prepared for two-hand playing; and it is well to select pieces in which the right and left hand parts are on the same level of difficulty.

As a preliminary exercise have the student play each part through a few times while you play the other part. It is important for him to read both parts and to listen to both parts though

94

he is playing only one. In this way he learns to integrate both parts mentally and feel the musical whole. He is prepared to read both parts together. This is quite different from the old method of practicing each hand alone unguided.

Drop the preliminary exercise of separate-hand playing as soon as possible. Urge your student to see the two staves as a whole, without allowing his eyes to shuttle up and down from one staff to the other. He should be careful also to strike both hands precisely together, never retarding the right hand.

Time values

Many beginners tend to release the keys too soon or too late, particularly when voices of different rhythmical divisions are to be combined in one hand. Instead of

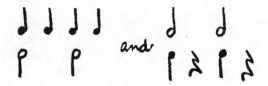

the pupil plays this way:

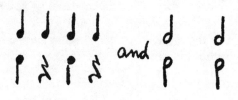

95

You may tolerate this inaccuracy until the pupil learns to understand polyphony. It will then help to have him play the polyphonic part of one hand with both his hands, distributing the voices between them, while you play the other part. For demonstration and exercise a reed organ (harmonium) should be used if it is available. It brings out polyphonic structure more clearly than does a piano.

Embellishments

Mordents, turns, and trills which are marked by signs may be left out by the student in his elementary period of sight-reading. Later have him play them by ear when they occur, following your accompaniment.

Rhythmical subdivision

In simple rhythms, your student can easily follow your accompaniment. In a complicated rhythmical subdivision, you may help him by adding a figure of uniform subdivision, as indicated in this example:

By subdivision the problem of *polyrhythm* can be solved, too. Use the common denominator of the unlike rhythms, as illustrated in the following examples:

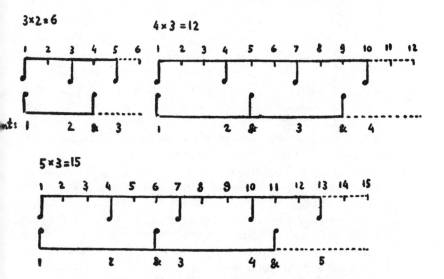

Charts of this kind help you play polyrhythms slowly enough for your pupil to follow your accompaniment; then all he need do to achieve correct rhythm is to strike note by note precisely with you. If he has trouble at first, you may have him play the parts separately but listen to the whole while you play it. Eventually he will feel and play polyrhythmic patterns as units.

We have discussed the stumbling blocks that pupils encounter in their elementary period of sight-reading. Though you as a teacher are ready to cope with these difficulties, even a responsive pupil will shrink from a new and troublesome task and may fail in his first attempts. At such times you may find it wise to drop the task temporarily; but take it up again at intervals. Eventually your pupil can handle any obstacle.

4. STUDY MATERIAL

According to the conventional teaching program, every pupil has to work out his pieces to some degree of perfection. A less talented beginner can accomplish this only with extremely easy pieces. Over-simplified study material is necessarily poor, dry, and rather monotonous. It cannot stimulate a pupil even if it is garnished with catchy titles, illustrations, and other trimmings. One of the first objectives of piano study should be to arouse the beginner's musical feelings, but no enthusiasm can be stimulated by musical baby-talk. From the beginning, the student's material should be rich in substance and variety. Such music confronts the beginner with greater initial difficulties. The difficulties, too, should increase more rapidly than in the conventional curriculum. Yet, as repeatedly stressed before, difficulty is a necessity rather than a disadvantage. It is the task of the teacher to help the pupil overcome difficulties, and a teacher, in properly guiding his pupil, has every chance of success.

The novice in sight-reading should be supplied with short pieces in which the difficulties are evenly distributed. Harsh dissonances should be avoided, but such challenges as sharps and flats, double-notes and chords, and a variety of harmonies and rhythms should be included. These problems should be presented to him at random rather than in classified order.

Elementary sight-reading material also should help the pupil cultivate good musical taste. Shallow or trashy music can spoil the beginner's taste and prevent him from developing appreciation for serious, valuable music. The best materials to start with are the folksongs of various nations. They offer a rich selection which meets all the demands of elementary sight-reading. Moreover, song is the natural beginning of music study, because the combination of words and melody brings the music closer to the beginner; this is particularly important for those with little musical experience.

From folksongs the pupil can graduate to the classics. He can, starting with simple tasks, work up to musical and pianistic complexities of any degree (see sight-reading program on pages 67–71).

5. Homework

As long as your student is entirely dependent upon your accompaniment he can practice only during lessons. This holds particularly for the period when he is reading with one hand at a time. After he has developed some facility in guided two-hand playing, have him play alone a little during each lesson under your supervision. Have him at first read a piece with you, then alone. Do not sit beside him or interrupt his playing for corrections. It will increase his self-confidence if, while he is playing alone, you will give him a minimum of help. Offer him criticism and suggestions only after he has finished his piece, and comment on his playing in general rather than dwell upon details.

Deprived of your accompaniment, he will fully reveal his weaknesses. Put up with them. What matters first is his independence as such, rather than his manner of solo-practicing. As soon as he has learned to sight-read tolerably well unguided, you may assign homework. Start him off right by playing the pieces with him. At home he may play them repeatedly, yet without aiming at perfection. Then have him play them again under your guidance.

After some practice he will be able to play pieces at sight unguided; then you may drop the preparatory work.

For a beginner a daily half-hour of sight-reading homework is sufficient to cover the necessary amount of music and to develop his facility. In a later study period a non-professional student may extend his practicing time to one hour a day.

Do not expect that your student's homework will help him to improve his working habits; for this purpose he has to keep on playing with you. Thus, his progress is the combined effect of both lessons and homework.

6. PLAYING BY EAR AND WRITTEN EXERCISES

Capable pupils may play by ear and do written exercises from the beginning, parallel to sight-reading work, while others should wait until they have become familiar with a considerable volume of music by sight-reading it.

With pupils who are ready, start by having them transpose from the page simple melodies and bass-parts into several keys. The easiest kind of transposition is from one key to another of the same notation: from 3 sharps to 4 flats, from 4 sharps to 3 flats, from 2 flats to 5 sharps, etc.

After the pupil has succeeded in transposing from notes, he may continue transposing from memory.

The next step is to combine melody and bass.

You may accompany the beginner, as he plays by ear, just as you guide his sight-reading. At home he should write down his attempts.

Written exercises for advanced students embrace the following:

Supplying melodies with full harmonies and polyphonies; re-arranging, simplifying or expanding piano pieces; arranging other instrumental music and vocal music for piano. Students who show some inventive ability may also attempt free composition.

Facility in playing by ear, by heart, and in improvisation develops out of these exercises.

Practicing by ear and written exercises require great effort and are time-consuming. Many students prefer to play from notes only. Even the more ambitious ones should spend only as much time on those exercises as they can afford without curtailing their regular piano work. You may decide in every individual case, according to the student's ability and willingness, if, when, and to what extent he should take up these exercises. After all, they are imperative only for the professional pianist, as they help him develop pianistic memory. An amateur can become a good musician without a memorized repertoire.

7. APPROACH TO CHILDREN

Any approach to the education of a child other than that of *unlimited optimism* is an injustice against him. Courage is contagious and so is pessimism. Let us joyously assume that any child can be taught to do anything that other human beings are able to do. If we are ignorant and mistaken in this view, we can damage no one by holding it. And the courage we imbibe from such a view is a sweeter brew than that of pessimism. The sublime "ignorance" of optimism alone accomplishes the "impossible." Let those who choose quibble over the limits of human potentialities.

> Marguerite and Willard Beecher
> (Individual Psychology Bulletin,
> Chicago, 1949, Vol. VII, p. 101)

By far the majority of piano pupils have been and still are of grammar-school age. Piano instruction was therefore adjusted to the mental and emotional immaturity of that age. Teachers usually set the rather limited goal that the child learn to perform a few easy pieces tolerably well. Many children could not accomplish even this; their studies ended in a little tragedy and nothing remained for them but unpleasant memories of the piano.

Children of today, brought up in greater liberty, rarely expose themselves to tragedies or boredom. Therefore, in order not to frighten away these modern children, many music teachers have reduced their standards. After all, they will say, a pupil does not have to show off, but plays for his own pleasure. Yet to play for pleasure calls for a fairly complete command of music and of the instrument, far more so than the mastery of a small repertoire required.

It certainly is unreasonable to torture and bore a pupil as teachers formerly did; this, however, does not mean that a pupil can be exempted from all difficulties. To help a pupil means to help him take the necessary steps in learning. Our sight-reading method makes necessary demands, and these, we must admit, are met more easily by a mature person than by a child. However, it will not help a child to be taught, even temporarily, in the conventional way, for that would not prepare him for sight-reading or for musical progress generally. Sight-reading is the best start for all pupils, including children. Only it takes a long while before the average child's efforts produce obvious results. This is not wasted time, for the child gets used to this routine, and little by little adjusts himself to the requirement of learning.

Ear training

A child who cannot repeat correctly a single tone which is played or sung to him may be considered unmusical. Before starting piano work, a child must learn to sing—to sing whole songs. Group work is the best training, where musical and unmusical children sing together, accompanied on the piano. Folksongs of all nations are the best material for beginners. The musical children will take the lead, while the others may remain silent at first or hum or mumble words rhythmically; yet they will continue to participate with increasing courage. Following the natural tendency and ability of children to imitate, sooner or later they will learn to sing properly.

Once a child's musical ear is awakened by singing, he can develop it to any degree by means of his piano work.

Special handicaps

Some children have unusual trouble grasping the idea of notation. This shortcoming is sometimes so pronounced that the pupil cannot recognize the relation of two notes in a row—whether they are alike or different, or which one is higher. This deficiency—provided the child's eyesight is physiologically normal—is merely functional: his attention focuses on only one note at a time.

Another deficiency is *left-eyedness;* it occurs mostly among left-handers. Left-eyedness can be tested by having the pupil take aim at a distant object with one eye; involuntarily he shuts his right eye. (A right-eyed person would shut his left eye.) The right eye tends naturally to read from left to right, while the left eye works in the opposite direction. If the pupil's left eye is dominant ("master eye") he will tend to read in reverse even when he employs both eyes. Left-eyed children have difficulties in their school-work too.

A left-eyed piano pupil has trouble reading ahead and integrating the notation into a whole. His difficulties increase when he tries to read the parts of both hands together.

Sometimes a left-eyed piano pupil develops skill through playing by ear, which proves conclusively that he is handicapped by his visual deficiency only. Some left-eyed beginners can overcome their initial difficulties more readily by putting a patch over the left eye while sight-reading.

Other children, though their eyes may read easily, lack motor coordination and finger memory. They have tremendous difficulty finding keys, establishing hand positions, and returning to them.

Many children have very sluggish mentalities in general; they are extremely slow in understanding the teacher's suggestions and in carrying them out.

Pupils with such handicaps at first fail entirely; they fumble badly, miss keys persistently, even when performing simple, repetitious figures. If these pupils, however, have a good musical ear and are ambitious to learn, it certainly is worth while to help them along. Their handicaps are caused by lack of training; sight-reading exercises help them make up for the training they have missed before. Their progress may be very slow but it will be steady.

Maturity level of the child

A pupil must be ready psychologically to accept his teacher's help; this maturity comes at different ages in different children, as all teachers know. There are children of four who respond immediately to instruction, and others of ten or more who completely ignore the teacher's suggestions. There are also gifted children who learn successfully by themselves, but obstruct their chances of advancement by balking at formal instruction.

Before you start giving lessons to a child of school or preschool age, ascertain the level of his maturity. Play a simple tune and have the child imitate you one octave higher or lower, while watching your fingers. Or, point one by one to the keys he should strike. This simple test shows you in a flash the child's attitude and mentality. One child will hesitate; he will look at you instead of the keyboard, and you may have to coax him to

104

strike each key note by note. Another will strike, but the wrong key. Still another will not wait for your help, but will strike keys haphazardly. A very young child sometimes pays no heed to your suggestions, but bangs along the whole keyboard, or asks questions, or runs away.

You may decide in every case whether you want to continue those attempts or reject the child. A child who shows a measure of willingness may be allowed to play by rote as a prelude to sight-reading, until he shows an adequate response to your instruction.

Ambition

Only very few children can muster the necessary ambition that sight-reading requires from the beginning. The average child does not want to exert himself. This is especially true of pampered children. A child changes his attitude frequently because of changes in external conditions. He may be, more or less, distracted by unrelated interests and events. Nor is it easy to win a child's cooperation in following his teacher's guidance. His readiness to cooperate depends greatly upon his personal relationship to the teacher.

Proceed slowly. Once in a while assign a more difficult piece to your pupil. Begin and end every lesson with some easy and pleasant assignment. Make the lessons short. Half an hour is ample for any child; for very young beginners even shorter lessons. Terminate a lesson as soon as your pupil gets tired. Assign homework to a child only if he is willing to do it. Before your pupil is ready for homework he should have had frequent lessons, lest his progress be too slow. If there must be longer intervals between the lessons, someone else can practice with the pupil in your place if he is patient enough with the pupil. Group work, however, is not feasible, as every pupil requires his own kind of guidance. Nor should beginners sight-read together unguided, because they confuse each other.

The most difficult pupil is one who is studying piano only because his parents want him to. To such a pupil, instruction looks like a set of vexatious demands goading him toward a goal not of his choosing. To work with his teacher means at best to do him a special favor. He follows your guidance listlessly if not reluctantly. He develops a lazy, slack, and sloppy manner of playing, guessing at the notes instead of reading them, striking keys haphazardly, disregarding rhythm, avoiding black keys, etc. He does not correct his mistakes and may even ignore your verbal corrections.

Never should a teacher be more ambitious for a pupil than the pupil is for himself, lest the teacher fall into the weak position of a creditor toward his insolvent debtor. The teacher's sole function is to help his pupil, and only to offer, never to force, his help upon him, for then help ceases to be help and becomes coercion. It places pupil as well as teacher under a constant strain. Tension and antagonism grow toward the inevitable parting.

It is useless to exert pressure upon an unambitious pupil. Put up with his attitude, let him play as he wants to, don't seek concrete results. This is the best way to await the turning point, for your own sake as well as for your pupil's sake.

From the teacher's angle, there is a fundamental asset in teaching a problem child: unlike an adult, a child can be coaxed along, even though he does not progress, so long as the teacher shows benevolence and friendliness. Sooner or later the pupil gets interested in the lessons, and once interest is kindled, by continuous work it may be fanned into enthusiasm.

It is very important to assure yourself of the cooperation of

106

your pupil's parents and guardians. They should not push or criticize the pupil, or in any other way interfere with your teaching or counteract it. Request them to wait for results with the same patience that you do. After all, a child has abundant time at his disposal—the time of unfolding maturity, which in itself is the teacher's best assistant.

With these problems of teaching children—they are the most difficult teaching problems—our scheme of rules and suggestions has come to its close. This scheme is meant as an outline only; the rules and suggestions are not exhaustive, nor can they be treated as rigid formulae; their application will result in as many variations as there are students.

A method which does not rely upon special talent must be adjustable to the varied peculiarities of students. In using such a method, the teacher learns from the failures of his students where his teaching needs improvement. Thus the worst learners among the pupils can become the best teachers of the instructor.

Our sight-reading method cannot be described completely in a book. But this book may encourage those of my colleagues who adopt the method to take supplementary lessons from their students.